A Rainbow of Reli

Christine Moorcroft

Stanley Thornes (Publishers) Ltd

1

Acknowledgements

The author and publisher would like to thank the children and staff of the following schools for help with displays:

Booker Junior School, Liverpool
Grange Primary School, Sefton
King David Primary School, Liverpool
Mosspits Junior School, Liverpool
Pinehurst Junior School, Liverpool
St Margaret's CE Infant School, Liverpool
St Margaret's CE Junior School, Liverpool

Thanks are also due to Jacque Emery (Inspector, Sefton Education Authority) and Joyce Wade (St Luke's Church and Religious Education Centre, Crosby, Merseyside).

Many of the religious artefacts and posters were kindly loaned by TTS Religion in Evidence, Monk Road, Alfreton, Derbyshire, DE55 7RL.

First published in 1998 by:
Stanley Thornes (Publishers) Ltd
Ellenborough House
Wellington Street
CHELTENHAM GL50 1YW
England

00 01 02 / 10 9 8 7 6 5 4 3 2

A catalogue record for this book is available from the British Library.
ISBN 0-7487-2952-6

Typeset by Aetos Ltd. Bathampton, Bath.
Illustrations by Aetos Ltd. Bathampton, Bath.
Printed and bound in China by Dah Hua Printing Press Co Ltd.

Contents

Introduction

A Rainbow of Religions provides a wealth of ideas to help teachers create displays of which they and their pupils can be proud. It shows how displays can be used to enhance the school environment and to promote learning. It suggests ways in which displays can help children to develop an appreciation of the cultures of the six major religions of the UK, while learning about each religion's scriptures, festivals and customs and developing an understanding of how faith affects people's lives. The book also presents ideas for displays based on general religious themes such as 'prayer', 'new baby', 'new life', 'wonderful world' and 'thank you'.

As required by the Education Reform Act 1988, *A Rainbow of Religions* presents religious education in a way that supports teachers in developing children's understanding of different faiths without attempting to inculcate a particular religious belief in the children. It recognises that children and teachers may be from a range of faith backgrounds or none at all. In accordance with the requirements of the Act, and following the recommendations of the School Curriculum and Assessment Authority, the emphasis of the book is on Christianity.

The displays are intended to: provide information about a religion; stimulate children's interest or encourage reflection; present children's writing or art in a way that shows it is valued; and provide a focus for learning. The displays can be used as visual stimuli during school or class assemblies. They can also pose questions for the children to consider. These questions can be factual or thought-provoking. At the end of an assembly the children could be asked to find out more about the topic or just to think about it. The displays can provide a focus for this.

The book is divided into seven sections that relate to the themes of most Locally Agreed Syllabuses: 'everyday life', 'lifetime', 'the natural world', 'festivals', 'people', 'special places' and 'books and stories'. Within each section there are some units of work that are not tied to a religion and others that are specific to one or other of the major religions. Each unit of work presents a display that can be either a starting point, or a continuous piece of work, or the culmination of the children's work. The teacher's planning is supported by guidance on the concepts to be developed, ideas for discussion, descriptions of the activities, details of the displays and a list of the resources required. Background information is provided where appropriate, and references are included to help the teacher.

The displays show how standard school materials can be combined to produce eye-catching effects. There are also ideas for using other easily available materials in creative ways - from wallpaper and gift-wrapping paper to scraps of fabric and even straw matting.

Consideration has been given to the choice of colours and style of lettering for the displays. Where appropriate, three-dimensional displays are created making use of such things as boxes, clothing, cut-out photographs and artificial flowers. Teachers will find uses for other 'recycled' materials they have collected, and they can adapt the ideas suggested here to enhance other topics in RE.

I believe

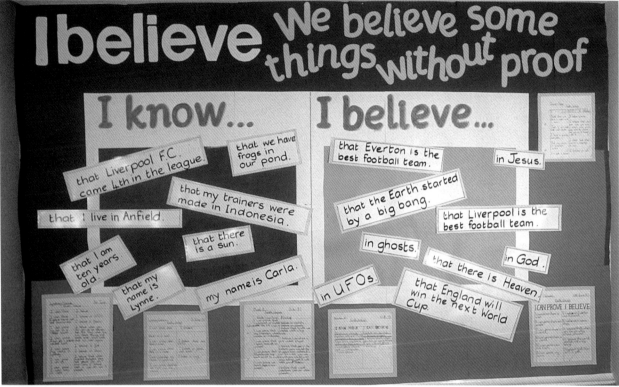

Discussion

Talk about things the children know and can prove to be true and those they believe to be true. What is the difference? Ask the children for examples. Do any of the children share the same beliefs? They could explain what makes them believe things that cannot be proved.

Activities

Working in groups of four, the children make charts on which they record things they can prove, and things they believe to be true.

Ask the children to read statements of belief from different faiths. Can they find any similarities and differences? Examples could include:

- The Apostles' Creed, one statement of Christian belief (*The Alternative Service Book*);
- The Shema, the central statement of faith for Jews (Deuteronomy 6: 4);
- The Mool Mantar, which expresses Sikh belief in God (this appears at the beginning of each chapter of the Guru Granth Sahib);
- An extract from *Rig Veda 1*, 16: 46, from the Hindu scriptures.

Display

The children talked about things they know and can prove to be true and things that they believe but cannot be proved. They chose some of their beliefs and knowledge, wrote them on to slips of paper and put them on the chart.

Concepts

Belief, faith

Resources

Blue and green backing paper; white paper; felt-tipped pens

The Five Pillars of Islam

Concepts

Belief, faith

Discussion

Ask the children to think of things they do every day such as cleaning their teeth, washing, or watching TV. Introduce the word 'routine' for things that are done regularly. Can the children think of other things they do at regular intervals - weekly, monthly, yearly?

In groups, or with the teacher, the children could decide which are the most important routines they have, and why. At this stage they may be thinking of practical routines, or activities they enjoy.

Activities

Make charts to show routines, using these headings: 'more than once a day', 'every day', 'every week', 'every month', 'every year'.

Introduce the Five Pillars of Islam with the help of a chart:

The Qur'an describes these routines as essential for Muslims. Ask the children how following the Five Pillars of Islam strengthens Muslims' belief in God. The children could write about how these routines help Muslims feel part of a religious community.

Display

Blue was chosen for the background because it is a colour often seen in mosques. Shapes of the windows and alcoves of mosques were cut from gold paper. To make the shapes symmetrical, sheets of gold paper were cut in half and half the shape was drawn on the reverse. Several thicknesses were cut at the same time and used as templates.

Resources

Dark blue backing paper; gold paper; plain postcards; direction compass; reference material about the Five Pillars of Islam

Important routines for Muslims			
More than once a day	**Every week**	**Every year**	**Once in a lifetime**
Say that God is the only God and Muhammad is his prophet (*Shahada*). Pray five times a day facing Makkah (*Salah*).	Give money to a collection at the mosque for people in need (*Zakah*).	Fast during the month of Ramadan (*Sawm*).	Make a pilgrimage to Makkah (*Hajj*).

Shahada
The words of the *Shahada* are shown in Arabic (in calligraphy and transliterated) and in English. The children wrote a sentence to show their own beliefs about God.

Salah
The children drew prayer mats and worked out the direction of Makkah from their classroom.

Zakah
The children listed people they think should be helped by *Zakah*. More lists show people who are allowed, in Islamic law, to receive it.

Sawm
The children drew pictures to show how they might feel if they fasted throughout the day for a whole month, and what they might do after each day's fast.

Hajj
The children wrote 'postcards home from Makkah' describing the *Hajj*. They drew pictures of the Ka'bah (the holiest building for Muslims, in Makkah) on the reverse of the postcards.

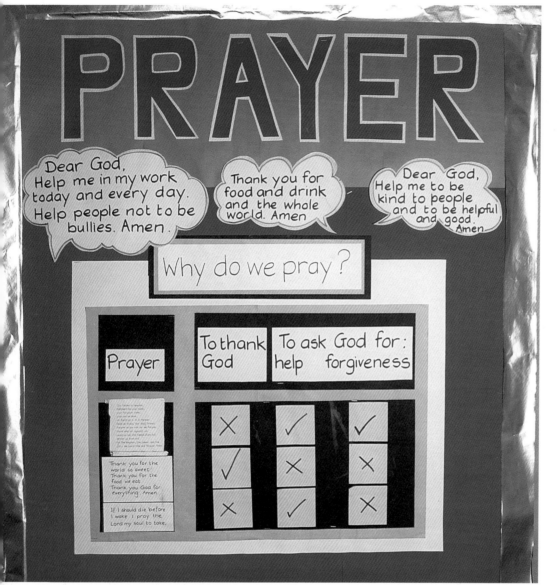

Concepts

What people do when they pray, why they pray and to whom they pray

Activities

Ask the children to write a prayer, carefully considering what the prayer is for and the words they will use.

Use a work of art as a starting point. A useful book is *A Child's Book of Prayer in Art* by Sister Wendy Beckett (Dorling Kindersley). Ask the children to look at the work of art. What kind of prayer does it make them think of? They could write a prayer inspired by the picture.

Discussion

Ask the children to bring in copies of any prayers they know. Provide a selection of prayers from Christianity and other faiths. Ask the class what each prayer is for. One prayer can have many purposes.

Ask the children what people do when they pray. They might close their eyes, kneel, sit, stand, touch their heads to the ground or sit cross-legged. They might use a rosary, prayer beads or a prayer mat, or face a particular direction. What would the children do if they prayed? Children who pray regularly could tell the others how they pray.

Display

The children made a chart to analyse prayers. In groups, they decided what the purpose of each prayer was and then put it into the appropriate section of the chart. They wrote prayers of their own for a particular purpose and copied out parts of these for the display.

Resources

Copies of prayers; prayer books - both Christian and from other faiths; a copy of a work of art that could inspire prayer

Sunday

Discussion

Ask the children to keep a diary for a weekday and a Sunday. Some children might be able to work out the time they spent on each activity and record this as a pie chart. What are the differences and similarities between their Sunday and their weekday activities?

Talk about why many businesses close on Sundays, with reference to the Sabbath Day described in the book of Exodus on which God forbade people to work, and the Sunday trading laws.

Resources

Purple backing paper; Sunday and weekday newspapers; history reference books showing Victorians in their 'Sunday best' or people in Tudor times being fined for not going to church on Sunday

Concept

Sunday as a special day for Christians, when they try to devote some time to prayer

Activities

Collect information about the weekday and Sunday opening times of local shops, supermarkets, libraries, offices, garages and other buildings. What do the children notice? Why do many buildings close on Sundays or have shorter opening hours? The children could use reference material to find out how Sunday trading has changed since Victorian or even Tudor times.

If possible, invite Christians to talk to the children about Sunday and what they do on that day which sets it apart from other days.

Display

A Sunday and a weekday newspaper were compared (to show how a Sunday paper has more pages because people have more time to read then). The children's Sunday and weekday diaries and pie charts were displayed, along with their research on Sunday trading. The purple background represents the colour of many church furnishings.

Shabbat

Background

Challot are plaited loaves which represent manna, the miraculous food that God sent to the Israelites in the desert (Exodus 16: 14-18). There are two *challot* because God told the Israelites to gather twice as much manna on the sixth day, so that they could rest on the seventh. The board under the *challot* and the cloth covering them symbolise the dew above and beneath the manna. Candles provide light, a symbol of God's presence. The smelling of spices ends Shabbat in a way that makes its memory linger. The *havdallah* candle has twelve wicks to symbolise the twelve tribes of Israel.

Concepts

Commemoration; symbolism

Discussion

Ask the children what they do on Saturdays and Sundays. How do these days differ from the other days of the week? What do the children know about the actions of religious people on these days?

Talk about work and leisure. The children could name work activities and leisure activities. Are there any that cause disagreement? Why?

Resources

Blue backing paper; artefacts used on Shabbat - menorah, candle with twelve wicks, goblets, *challot* and cover; reference books about Judaism

Activities

Provide the children with 'diary format' pages so that they can make a note of the activities they do on weekdays and on Saturdays and Sundays.

The children could find out about the activities that Jews are allowed/not allowed to do on Shabbat and record these on a chart.

Show the children the artefacts used on Shabbat and explain their significance. Provide *challot* to taste and spices to smell.

Display

The Shabbat artefacts were kindly loaned by TTS Religion in Evidence. The border consists of stencilled symbols of Judaism - the Star of David and the *menorah*. A blue background was chosen to symbolise the blue star on the flag of Israel.

The Five Ks

Concepts

The importance of outward symbols in the expression of belief, especially in Sikhism

Discussion

Ask the children to bring to school badges they wear. Which are their most important badges? Why? They could look in magazines for pictures of people wearing badges or symbols (perhaps on uniforms). What can the children find out about people from the badges or symbols they wear in everyday life?

Show the children the symbols worn by Sikhs and talk about their significance. How does a Sikh feel when he or she puts on one or more of the Five Ks? Of what might these symbols remind him or her?

Read the story of Guru Gobind Singh and the founding of the Khalsa - it explains the origins and symbolism of the Five Ks and of Sikhism.

Activities

The children could draw badges they have collected and make a display. Ask them to describe their own special badge. What makes it special? Perhaps it reminds them of something.

The children could find out more about the Five Ks, then draw one and say why it is special. Some of the Five Ks are adapted for wearing in everyday life - the *kirpan* (dagger) is often represented as a badge. The children could write about when it might be difficult for a Sikh to wear one of the symbols, e.g. the *kara* (bracelet) in sports.

Display

The display conveys the 'flavour' of Sikhism as well as giving information. Gold paper and gold/orange chiffon material were used to reflect the colour traditionally associated with Sikhism. The artefacts were kindly loaned by TTS Religion in Evidence.

Resources

Artefacts - the Five Ks, the *Khanda* (symbol of Sikhism) and the *Nishan Sahib* (Sikh flag); the children's own badges; magazines; gold paper; gold/orange chiffon

Puja

Display

The display represents the kind of shrine found in many Hindu homes. It includes pictures and statuettes of Hindu deities, symbolic artefacts used during *puja* (worship) and offerings. Hindu home shrines are decorated in a way that makes them special and different from the rest of the home. It should be stressed that the display is not a shrine - its purpose is to show how Hindus worship.

Concepts

Devotion, a special place in the home for worship

Resources

Books about Hinduism; pictures and statuettes of Hindu deities; fruit and flowers; a metal tray with bell, oil lamp, incense burner, incense, water pot, spoon and sandalwood paste

Discussion

Use the display as a starting point. Small groups of children could look at, handle, smell and taste some of the objects. Ask the children how the objects make the area different from the rest of the classroom. How could the objects be used to create a special 'feel' while people are praying?

Activities

Explain that worshippers begin by letting the deity know they are going to pray. Then they need something to show they are praying, something to make the air pleasant, something with which to wash and refresh the deity, something to use for offering the deity food, something to make a special spot on their forehead and on the deity's, and offerings to make the deity happy. Ask the children which items might be used for each purpose and why. The children could draw and write their responses.

Life and growth

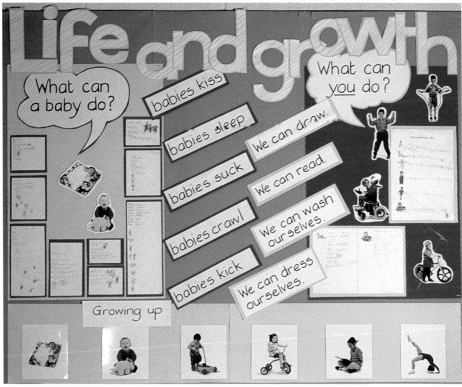

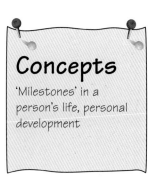

Concepts

'Milestones' in a person's life, personal development

Discussion

Ask the children to name some of the things a baby can do. What can they themselves do? The children could describe how they have changed since they were babies. Which of their achievements have been celebrated?

Activities

Provide pictures of children from birth through to the children's present age. Ask the children to put the pictures in order. How did they decide on the order? Provide pictures of items such as a baby's feeding bottle, a teething ring and toys for children of different ages. Ask the children to match the objects to the pictures of children who might use them.

The children could make books about their lives so far. Ask them to collect photographs of themselves and other memorabilia such as their identity tags if they were born in hospital, baptism certificates and so on. These could be fixed into the books (or photographs of them glued in).

Display

The bright green and yellow symbolise growth. The children cut out pictures of children of their own age and babies, then they drew and wrote about things they can do and things a baby can do. Some of their ideas were copied out by the teacher for the class to read together. The children made a timeline along the bottom by putting in order pictures of children of different ages. The pictures are from *Getting Personal: Beginning Personal, Social and Health Education* (Folens 1997).

Resources

Yellow, green and red backing paper; pictures of children of different ages; pictures of toys, computers and baby equipment

New baby

Concepts

Awareness of the idea of preparation for, and the feeling of celebration at, the arrival of a new baby

Discussion

Show the children a picture of a new baby and ask them what they can tell you about it. How might each person in a family feel when he or she hears there is to be a new baby? Show the children 'new baby' greetings cards and read out the words. Which do the children like best? Why?

Ask the children what a family has to do to get ready for a new baby. Talk about the changes that might have to be made in the home. Talk about gifts for a baby. Read the story of *Sleeping Beauty* and talk about the gifts her fairy godmothers gave her.

Display

'New baby' wrapping paper was used for part of the background and the heading. The children cut out pictures of baby equipment and clothes and glued these on to card. Baby equipment, toys and clothes were brought in from home.

Activities

The children could write about how families prepare for a new baby, using the headings: 'things to do', 'things to buy', 'how people feel'.

Ask the children to paint pictures of how people celebrate the birth of a baby. They could design their own 'new baby' wrapping paper, perhaps using a computer.

The children could look at 'new baby' greetings cards, noting the objects that are often shown on them. They could make their own cards with cut-out pictures from used cards and their own messages.

Resources

A large picture of a baby; 'baby' wrapping paper; 'new baby' cards; outgrown baby equipment, toys and clothes

Birth ceremony

Background

The Call to Prayer:
'Allah is most great.
There is no God but Allah and Muhammad is His Prophet.
Come to prayer. Come to success.
Allah is most great.
There is no God but Allah.'

Concepts

Welcoming babies into the Muslim faith; the Call to Prayer

Activities

The children could write about the earliest thing they remember hearing. What makes them remember it?

Display

A blue background represents the colour often associated with Islam. The children wrote their important messages for a baby in large letters. These were mounted in speech bubbles around the picture of the Muslim father and baby. The picture is from *Photopack: Islam* (Folens 1995).

Discussion

Show the children a picture of a new-born baby. What beliefs would they like a baby to have? Ask the children to write a message that they would whisper in a new-born baby's ear.

Resources

Blue backing paper; felt-tipped pens; a copy of the Qur'an; the words of the adhan in English, transliterated Arabic and Arabic calligraphy

Read the words of the *adhan* (Call to Prayer) in English, emphasising the first word (Allah). Tell the children that when a Muslim baby is born the father whispers these words in the baby's ear, while honey is put on the baby's tongue. What will be the first word the baby hears? Why is honey given? If the children were to taste sweetness while doing something, would they have good or bad memories of the action? Talk about the importance to Muslims of bringing up their children in their faith and how the birth ceremony is the start of this.

Baptism

Discussion

Have the children been to a baptism? Ask them to describe what happened. Can they remember anything the minister said during the service? The service of infant baptism refers to the 'new family' the child joins - do the children know what this is? They could find out from the words of the baptism service: 'God takes you for His own child and all Christian people to be your brothers and sisters'.

Light a baptismal candle and talk about light as a symbol of Jesus, 'the Light of the World'. Have the children any idea what this might mean? The words of John 3: 18-21 describe evil people as those who prefer darkness because it hides their evil deeds. Honest men come to the light so that 'it may be clearly seen that God is in all they do'.

Do the children know the name of the special part of the church that contains the water for baptism? (The font.) Read parts of the baptism of infants service and ask the children what promises the godparents make on behalf of the child.

> '
> ... when you are baptised, you become a member of a new family.
>
> God takes you for His own child and all Christian people will be your brothers and sisters.'

Activities

Show a video recording of a Christian baptism and ask the children to write an account of it. Alternatively, ask a local Christian minister to perform a mock baptism, using a doll. The children could help to organise the event, choose names, godparents and so on.

Provide dictionaries of first names from a range of cultures so that the children can find the meaning of their own names and the ones they might choose for a baby. They could also look at baptismal greetings cards and notice the symbols that appear on them.

Children who have baptism certificates could bring these to school. The children could look for similarities and differences between their certificates, which could be photocopied for display. Baptism photographs could also be displayed. The children could draw or write about any special clothes they wore and presents they received.

Read the biblical account of the baptism of Jesus by John the Baptist:

> But John tried to make him change his mind. 'I ought to be baptised by you,' John said, 'and yet you have come to me!'
> But Jesus answered him, 'Let it be so for now. For in this way we shall do all that God requires.' So John agreed.
> As soon as Jesus was baptised, he came up out of the water. Then heaven was opened to him, and he saw the Spirit of God coming down like a dove and alighting on him. Then a voice said from heaven, 'This is my own dear Son, with whom I am pleased.' (Matthew 3: 14-17, *Good News Bible*)

Parts of this may be difficult for some children to understand, but ask them why they think John tried to turn Jesus away. How was Jesus' baptism special? The dove was a special sign - of what? (Peace)

(Baptism is symbolic of washing away sin and beginning a new life in God's grace through the forgiveness of sins. Baptism of infants is therefore much more than a naming ceremony.)

Display

Silver featured in the display because of the silver gifts traditionally given at christenings. Artefacts associated with infant baptism such as a white christening gown, hat and shoes, gifts, a 'baptism pack' from a church, a baptismal candle, and baptism certificates were collected and displayed.

Resources

The words of the Christian baptism service from *The Alternative Service Book* (HarperCollins Religious/CUP 1980); silver paper; art paper; artefacts connected with baptism

17

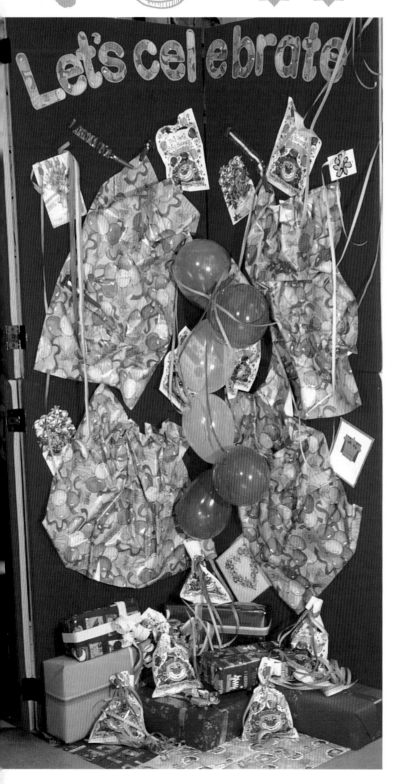

Discussion

Ask the children to name some events that they celebrate. Ask them what they are celebrating. Most celebrations commemorate an event in the past - the date of someone's birth, an important event in a community, or significant events in the life of a key person.

How often do the children celebrate a particular occasion? Most celebrations are annual, on the anniversary of the event to be celebrated.

How do the children celebrate? They might send cards, eat special foods, wear special clothes, decorate their homes and other buildings, give presents, exchange visits, share a special meal with others, or have special symbols or rituals such as blowing out candles, having a Christmas tree or Advent calendar, lighting candles or other lamps, playing certain games, or going to a place of worship.

Resources

Gift-wrapping paper; backing paper; greetings cards; party invitations; 'goody' bags; paper hats; streamers; balloons; party novelties; decorations; party games

Activities

In groups, the children could plan the celebration of an event connected with the school. Each group could present its celebration plan to the whole class, and then decide the best way to celebrate and why. If possible, carry out the children's planned celebration on the appropriate date. The children could design invitations to their celebration - what information will they need to include? They could design commemorative paper hats and T-shirts too.

Display

The display is intended as a starting point to create the feeling of celebration. The children chose their favourite gift-wrapping paper, which was 'scrunched' and arranged on a bright background. Then they suggested items that should be included. The lettering was cut from gift-wrapping paper.

Concepts

Celebration of special events; making a day special

18

Bar/Bat Mitzvah

Discussion

Talk about commitments the children make when they join an organisation such as Brownies, Cubs, a swimming club or an orchestra. The children might have found it difficult to attend all the meetings of their group if they wanted to play with friends instead. They could talk about groups they have left because the commitments were too difficult to keep. The children could think of ways to help one another keep commitments. How do they feel when they have kept their commitments?

Activities

Provide reference material so that the children can find out about the commitment a Jewish boy or girl makes for his Bar or her Bat Mitzvah ceremony.

Concepts

Special times in an individual's life; making a commitment to a faith

The children could look at Bar and Bat Mitzvah cards and find out what the Hebrew words say. Help them to identify the symbols on the cards, such as the Torah, scrolls, *tallit* (prayer shawls) and *tephillin* (leather boxes containing a copy of the Shema, which are fastened to the forehead and arm).

Resources

Bar and Bat Mitzvah cards; blue and gold paper

Display

In groups, the children made timelines of their special occasions or 'milestones'. They researched the significance of the Bar/Bat Mitzvah ceremony; they copied some of the Hebrew words used in the ceremony and found out what they meant. The blue background is the colour of the star on the flag of Israel. The children used card templates to make the gold shapes, which represent the symbols of Judaism.

The Hajj

Discussion

Ask the children about special journeys they have made and the reasons for them.

Use the display to help the children find out about the significance of the Hajj and the events that take place during the journey.

Background

'Hajj' is the fifth pillar of Islam (see pages 6-7). It commemorates the story of Ibrahim (Abraham), his wife Hajjar (Haggar) and his son Isma'il (Ishmael), which is told in the Qur'an (2: 124-147, 11: 69-73, 15: 51-56, 51: 24-30, 37: 99-111). In the biblical version of this story, the son whom Abraham was willing to sacrifice was said to be Isaac, not Ishmael.

Muslims who can afford to do so are required to make the pilgrimage to Makkah (Mecca) at least once in their lives. They wear *ihram* (plain white clothing) to show that they are leaving behind worldly cares in order to focus on the spiritual purpose of the journey. During the Hajj the pilgrims do not cut their hair or fingernails, nor do they wear jewellery, perfume or cosmetics. These symbolic actions help to eliminate material differences between the people on the Hajj, emphasising the Muslim belief that all people are equal in the eyes of God. The Hajj usually takes place during the month of *Dhul-Hijjah*.

Display

The posters provided reference material for the children's study of the Hajj. The children drew outlines of each other lying on paper. Then they cut out some of these life-sized figures and dressed them as *hajjis* or *hajjas* (male or female pilgrims).

Activities

The children could use atlases to find the location of Makkah. Then they could find out about the journey to get there. They could write about the preparations for the journey.

Help the children to make pictorial maps to show the actions of the pilgrims on the Hajj in the appropriate locations:

- *wudu* (symbolic washing);

- removing jewellery and putting on *ihram*;

- *tawaf* (walking seven times, clockwise, round the Ka'bah - see page 54);

- *sa'y* (walking quickly seven times between two small hills in Makkah called Safa and Marwah), which symbolises the search for water in the desert by Hajjar and Isma'il;

- camping overnight on the plain of Arafat, just outside Makkah, where they perform *zuhr* (midday prayer) and *asr* (late afternoon prayer);

- travelling after sunset to Mina, where they throw stones at three pillars to commemorate the stoning of Iblis (the devil) by Ibrahim;

- paying for a sheep or goat to be killed to commemorate the sacrifice that Ibrahim was prepared to make to show his faith in God;

- cutting their hair and/or nails to show that the pilgrimage is over, before again walking round the Ka'bah.

When someone dies

Discussion

Have any children had a pet that died? What did they do with its body? Why? Talk about the feelings they had, and how they gradually stopped being sad. Did they do anything to help them remember what their pet was like when it was alive? How did it help?

Talk about people dying. What do people do when someone close to them dies? What might they do to mourn the death and celebrate that person's life?

In groups, the children could talk about how people's bodies should be treated after death. They could find out about death ceremonies from Christianity and other faiths.

Take the children for a walk around a Christian cemetery (tell them beforehand that a cemetery is a peaceful place and should be treated with respect).

The children could copy or make rubbings of some inscriptions (permission should be sought first). Ask the children to notice the words that people use on gravestones. Why do people put carved headstones on graves and why do they put flowers there?

Activities

Read *Badger's Parting Gifts* by S Varley (Collins 1984). The story is about an old badger who tries to prepare his friends for his death by telling them not to be sad, but to remember the happy times they shared. But his friends are sad until they start talking about their memories of him. Ask the children how Badger helped his friends cope with their sadness when he died. The children could write and draw their happy memories of someone who has died.

For older or more able children, read excerpts from the Christian burial service in *The Alternative Service Book* (HarperCollins Religious/CUP 1980). Do the words say that death is the end of the person? Are there words suggesting new life? Remind the children of Jesus' death. Ordinary people do not rise from the grave, but how can they have a new life?

Jesus said, 'I am the resurrection, and I am the life; he who believes in me, though he die, yet shall he live, and whoever lives and believes in me shall never die.' (John 11: 25-26)

God so loved the world that He gave His only Son, that whoever believes in Him should not perish, but shall have eternal life. (John 3: 16)

We believe that Jesus died and rose again; and so it will be for those who died as Christians; God will bring them to life with Jesus. Thus we shall always be with the Lord. Comfort one another with these words. (Thessalonians 4: 14-18)

May God in His infinite love and mercy bring the whole Church, living and departed in the Lord Jesus, to a joyful resurrection and the fulfilment of His eternal kingdom. Amen. (Funeral service in *The Alternative Service Book*)

Display

The background was made from wax-crayon rubbings taken from gravestones. The black fabric drape represents the traditional mourning colour in Christianity. Artificial flowers were included because the children noticed that people often placed flowers on people's graves.

Resources

Black and purple backing paper; black fabric; artificial flowers; white paper; wax crayons

Discussion

Explain to the children the Muslim belief about what happens to people when they die: during life everyone is watched over by two angels who record everything he or she does; then at the moment of death, the person is judged. His or her 'good' deeds are balanced against the 'bad' ones. If good prevails, the person's spirit enters heaven to be with Allah.

The children could talk about their ideas of heaven. Do they believe in it and what might it be like? Some children could look at whether other faiths believe in heaven or in life after death. How might these beliefs influence what people do?

Resources

Dark blue backing paper; white art paper; gold backing paper; thick felt-tipped pens; reference material about Islam and other faiths; a copy of the Qur'an

Concept

Death in Islam: judgement of a person, in terms of 'good' and 'bad' deeds, at the end of his or her life

Activities

In groups, the children could list 'good' and 'bad' actions and put them in order - from 'good' to 'best' and from 'bad' to 'worst'. Using reference material, the children could find out and write about ideas of 'good' and 'bad' in Islam and compare these with their own ideas. Encourage the children to think about the reasons for some of the rules of Islam.

Display

The children were asked to think about how the 'balance' between good and bad deeds could be depicted. The result was a pair of scales that has 'good' deeds on one side and 'bad' on the other.

New life

Discussion

Ask the children to describe the regular events in nature that happen in particular seasons, such as trees shedding their leaves in autumn. Why do these events happen at these times? Talk about animal life-cycles in the same way. Why are lambs born in spring? Why do hedgehogs hibernate in winter?

Resources

Yellow, green and red backing paper; white art paper; paints; wide felt-tipped pens; pictures of animal and plant life-cycles

Activities

Provide pictures from the life-cycles of some plants and animals that cannot be observed. Which picture comes first? The children's answer might be 'the egg' or 'the seed'. Ask the children where the egg or seed came from. Help them to arrange the pictures in a circle to show this.

Display

The children's work and photographs of life-cycles were mounted on brightly-coloured paper and put on to a yellow background. The heading was made by drawing large letters on paper where green and yellow parallel lines had been ruled. The letters were glued on to green paper and cut out to leave a small border. The children cut out frogs and gave them folded-paper 'concertina' legs.

Questions that encouraged the children to think about the miracle of new life were displayed and changed from time to time. The class tried to find the answers to the new questions. Soon the children began to think of their own questions.

Concepts

The cycles of events in the natural world; the wonder of nature

Discussion

Can the children imagine a time when nothing existed? Ask them to imagine and describe the scene before the world was created - sights, sounds, and smells. If they had to begin creating something from that, what would the children do first?

If any children know the biblical account, they could tell the others what God did first when he created the world. Read the story from a children's Bible or tell the story of Genesis 1.

Display

The silver background has a border cut from gift-wrapping paper with a 'fruit and flower' design. The heading was cut from navy-blue card (to represent the dark blue space that the children thought existed before the world was created) and the children's writing and drawings were mounted on the same colour.

Concept
God as Creator

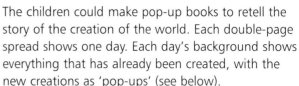

Activities

The children could paint and write about the scene before the Creation. Using 'thought bubbles,' they could add God's thoughts about what he was going to do first.

Ask the children to think of five things that make them wonder why God created those things. They might choose things such as spiders, wasps, bad smells, unkind people and earthquakes. Their challenge is to suggest an explanation for each one.

Seven groups of children could each plan and enact a different day of the Creation. They could perform these, in order, for another class or for a whole-school assembly. During the performance of each day's Creation, ask the audience what is being created. If nothing is being created, ask the audience why, and what is God doing?

The children could make pop-up books to retell the story of the creation of the world. Each double-page spread shows one day. Each day's background shows everything that has already been created, with the new creations as 'pop-ups' (see below).

Resources

Silver backing paper; navy-blue card; 'fruit and flower' design wrapping paper; a Bible or a children's Bible; A4 paper; scissors; glue

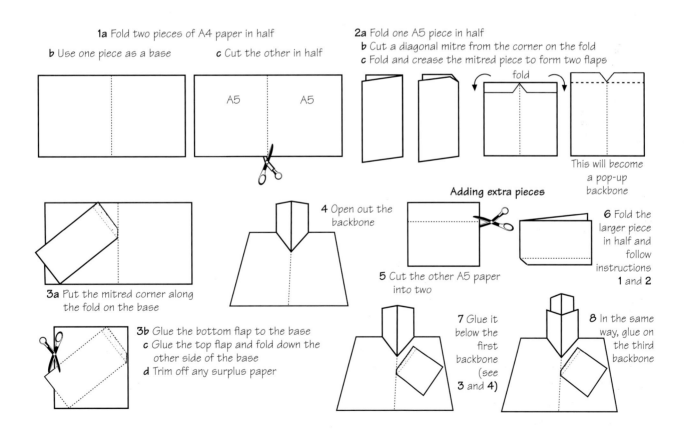

1a Fold two pieces of A4 paper in half
 b Use one piece as a base
 c Cut the other in half

A5　　A5

2a Fold one A5 piece in half
 b Cut a diagonal mitre from the corner on the fold
 c Fold and crease the mitred piece to form two flaps

fold

This will become a pop-up backbone

3a Put the mitred corner along the fold on the base

3b Glue the bottom flap to the base
 c Glue the top flap and fold down the other side of the base
 d Trim off any surplus paper

4 Open out the backbone

Adding extra pieces

5 Cut the other A5 paper into two

6 Fold the larger piece in half and follow instructions 1 and 2

7 Glue it below the first backbone (see 3 and 4)

8 In the same way, glue on the third backbone

Wonderful world

Discussion

Do the children know the difference between natural materials and objects and manufactured ones? They could sort pictures into two sets: 'natural' and 'made by people'.

Ask the children to close their eyes and imagine a beautiful natural scene. Invite them to describe their beautiful scenes.

Resources

A small container such as an egg box or ice cream tub for each child; magazines; a selection of papers and fabrics

Display

The children examined materials such as wallpaper, gift-wrapping paper, mounting paper and fabrics, and chose for the display background the ones they thought looked 'natural'. Magazines were provided so that the children could cut out and collect pictures of beautiful natural objects, which they then glued on to the 'natural' backgrounds.

Activities

Provide each child with a small container so that he or she can collect 'beautiful natural things' during a nature walk in the school grounds.

Concept

The beauty of the natural world

To add interest to the activity, the children could be given a list of things to collect such as something 'beautiful and shiny and green', 'delicate and red', 'small and purple', 'white and pointed', and so on.

Encourage the children to bring in beautiful natural things from home (with permission). They could write a poem entitled 'Something beautiful'.

The children could find poems, songs and hymns about beauty in nature. They could then choose their favourite one to learn, copy out for the display and perform during a class or school assembly.

Loy Kratong

Background

The festival of Loy Kratong celebrates the life of the Buddha. On rivers or lakes Buddhists float real or imitation lotus flowers, into which are fixed incense sticks and candles. Lotus flowers are a symbol of spiritual growth and enlightened minds.

Discussion

Have the children seen a lotus flower? Show them a real flower or look at pictures. Make sure they notice that the flowers grow above the water while the roots extend down to the murky depths.

Show the children pictures of Loy Kratong. Talk about the flower symbolising the idea that people can grow spiritually and become enlightened whatever their surroundings, just as the lotus can flower on top of murky or polluted water. What might Buddhists think and feel as they float their flowers on the water? How might the incense and the light of the candles help people in their prayers?

Display

The blue paper represents a river with green for its banks. The heading is cut from floral design wallpaper. There are tissue paper lotus flowers with paper candles glued to their centre. The children's prayers are displayed as if floating away on the water.

Activities

Make lotus flowers to float in bowls of water (see below).

Ask the children to compose a prayer for someone who wants to live a good life despite what is going on around him or her. The children could add lotus flower borders to their prayers.

Resources

Blue and green backing paper; coloured paper; tissue paper; glue; scissors; plastic bowls; cake candles and holders (for the floating flowers)

1 Draw a smaller circle on circular piece of card

2 Cut out petals from pink and white paper

fold

tab

3 Curl petals by running the edge of scissors blade along them

4 Glue petals all around smaller circle then around edge

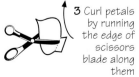

The Buddha and the swan

Concept

Appreciation of Buddhist values: that living things should not be harmed (the first of the Five Moral Precepts of Buddhism)

Story

Prince Siddattha lived in Northern India in a splendid palace with beautiful gardens.

One day he was walking near to a stream full of lotus flowers when a wounded swan fell at his feet. It had an arrow through its wing. The prince gently pulled out the arrow and comforted the bird.

He was wondering who had done this wicked thing when his cousin Devadatta came rushing out of the trees. 'That's mine, not yours,' he shouted. 'I shot it. Give it back to me.' Devadatta had been out hunting, as was expected of young men of noble birth. 'No,' Siddattha replied, 'I will not give this beautiful creature to you, so that you can do it more harm.'

The two cousins argued; neither would give in. They asked a wise man to judge who should keep the swan. After thinking very carefully, the wise man said that it was better to give life than to take it and so Prince Siddattha should have the swan. The prince cared for the bird until it recovered and then he set it free.

Resources

Sky-blue backing paper; various shades of green paper; white paper; 'feathers' cut from white paper; 'lotus flowers' cut from pale pink paper (see page 29); paint; leaves; wax crayons

Discussion

Ask the children what the story tells them about Prince Siddattha, Devadatta and the wise man.

Tell the children that Prince Siddattha was later known as the Buddha and his actions in this story show one of the Five Moral Precepts (rules) of Buddhism: Buddhists must promise not to harm living things. Ask the children to imagine what this would mean in everyday life. They could think about living things that are harmed by people: animals that are eaten; animals that are hunted; insects (by swatting them or using insect-killing sprays); snails and slugs (killed by gardeners' slug pellets); old dogs and horses that are taken to the vet to be put down.

Tell the children that most Buddhists are vegetarians, but some are not. How can Buddhists eat meat if they have promised not to harm living things? (Many Buddhists accept that animals are killed for food anyway - whether or not they eat them - and because of this Buddhists are not responsible for their deaths.)

Activities

Ask the children to imagine first that they are Devadatta, then Prince Siddattha, trying to convince the wise man that they should have the swan. They should remember that hunting was a normal activity for rich young men, who were learning the skills they would later need to be great warriors. The children could draw Devadatta and Siddattha, with speech bubbles to show what each might say to the wise man. Next to a picture of the wise man they could write thought bubbles to show what he might have been thinking when making up his mind.

The children could write their own stories about characters who care about living things. They could paint a scene from their story.

Display

Lotus flowers were made from pale pink paper, and feathers were cut from white paper, which was then curled using scissors:

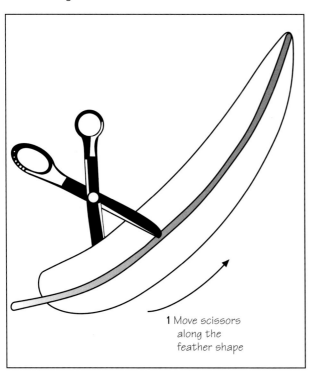

1 Move scissors along the feather shape

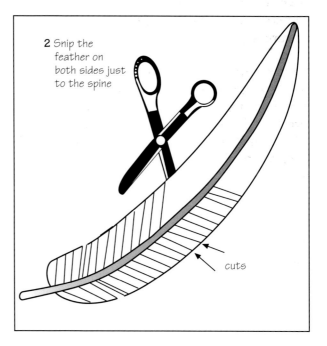

2 Snip the feather on both sides just to the spine

cuts

The petals and feathers, together with pictures of the main characters (painted by the children), were mounted on a sky-blue background. The border was cut from floral gift-wrapping paper. Cut-out leaf rubbings made by the children were added, together with leaf outlines cut from shades of green paper.

People and animals

Discussion

Ask the children: 'Should people kill animals?' The class is likely to be divided on this. Invite children to explain their answer. The fact is that people do, legally, kill animals. Can the children explain why? In groups, they could list legal reasons for killing animals. Are there any laws that they think should be changed? Remind them that reptiles, fish, birds, insects and other creepy-crawlies are animals. The children should consider what might happen if no insects were killed. They should also bear in mind that animals eat other animals.

What do the children think should be done about animals that kill people? Open the discussion with a news report of an incident such as the killing of a human by a dog, wild animal, or zoo animal, omitting any reference to the consequences for the animal. Let the children decide what should happen.

Concept

Care of living things, particularly animals

Activities

Ask the children to think about animals that are friends to people. They could describe an incident that shows an animal helping a human. To encourage empathy, ask them to write from the animal's point of view. They could write on animal-shaped pieces of paper.

The children could write their own poems based on 'Hurt No Living Thing' by Christina Rossetti.

Display

A green background was chosen to represent nature. A poster featuring Christina Rossetti's poem was displayed. The poster is from *Infant RE Book 1 Pack* (Stanley Thornes). The children cut out and collected pictures of animals and arranged them in groups on the display. The heading was cut from a wallpaper border with an animal design.

Resources

Green backing paper; an enlarged copy of the poem 'Hurt No Living Thing'; pictures of animals; 'animal' wallpaper border in bright colours

Hurt No Living Thing

Hurt no living thing
Ladybird, nor butterfly
Nor moth with dusty wing.
Nor cricket chirping cheerily,
Nor grasshopper so light of leap,
Nor dancing gnat, nor beetle fat,
Nor harmless worms that creep.

Christina Rossetti

Khilafah

Background

'Khilafah' means 'stewardship'. Muslims believe that Allah entrusted his creation to people, who are his stewards and have a duty to take care of the world and everything in it.

Concepts

Stewardship (in Islam); people as stewards of God's creation

Discussion

Ask the children who they think is responsible for taking care of their classroom, bedroom, home, town or city, country and the Earth. Record their responses. Which organisations or groups have they named? What are their own responsibilities for caring for each of these places?

Read the following parts of the Qur'an about people as God's stewards:

'Behold,' thy Lord said to the angels, 'I will create a vice-regent on Earth.' (2:30)

It is He who hath made you His agents, inheritors of the Earth. (6:165)

Mankind, inheritors of the Earth. (28:62)

Can the children explain why, according to the Qur'an, God makes people his stewards?

Why does God need stewards and what must they do?

Ask the children to think of something special they have made. If they allowed others to use it, how would they make sure it was kept safe?

Activities

Help the children organise a survey of their locality to find out how well different parts of it are cared for, and by whom. They could collect data about how these areas are looked after and the actions that damage them, and record their findings on a chart.

Display

The display represents a tree in a field. On the leaves the children wrote down what people should do to be good stewards of God's creation.

Resources

Green backing paper in various shades; brown paper; large leaf-shapes cut from pale paper

33

Thank you

Discussion

Ask the children to name things for which they are thankful. Compile a list on a large piece of paper, flip-chart or chalk-board, encouraging every child to contribute. For which things on the list have they actually said 'thank you'? Read through the list, asking the children to suggest why they should say thank you for the others. Did they forget? Did they know whom to thank?

Concept
Expressing thanks

Display

The children wrote prayers of thanks, and poems that they would like to send to people to say 'thank you' for something special. The background was made from gift-wrapping paper; the border was made from plain paper in one of the colours of the wrapping paper. The headings were cut from plain paper.

Resources

Brightly patterned gift-wrapping paper; backing paper in colours that match the gift-wrapping paper; 'thank you' cards

Activities

The children could make charts to show what they are thankful for, whom they should thank and how. They could write poems entitled 'Thank you'.

Collect and display 'thank you' cards. Ask the children to do a survey of the different kinds of pictures found on them. They could record the results on a graph or database to identify the most popular image found on 'thank you' cards.

The children could list the occasions for which people might send 'thank you' cards and add this information to their database.

In groups, ask the children to discuss and list the ways in which people give thanks to God, e.g. with prayers, songs and hymns; by making donations at a place of worship or to charity; or by helping others. They could write their own prayers of thanks.

Harvest

Discussion

Ask the children what 'harvest' means. They may be familiar with its connection with food, but can they think of other things people need that are produced or brought to them by the hard work of other people? Examples include: fresh water, fuel, and clothes.

Activities

Begin with the words of the hymn 'We Plough the Fields and Scatter'. The children could sort some of the ideas in the hymn, using a chart:

People work	God provides	People give thanks for	God's wishes
plough	water	all good gifts	humble, thankful hearts
scatter seeds	warmth	all things bright and good	
	breezes	seed-time	

The children could add information to their charts as they read the words of this hymn and others. They could look for words that suggest another kind of harvest - God's harvest of Christian people.

Display

The children made a 'harvest' collage, using pictures of foods such as fruit, vegetables, grains and bread. Each piece was glued on to a pale background, cut out and then glued on to dark brown paper. The heading was drawn using wooden letter templates and then cut from magazine pages.

Resources

Gift-wrapping paper or wallpaper with a 'harvest' pattern; brightly-coloured, plain backing paper; hymn books; magazines

The Annunciation

Background

Although the Annunciation is celebrated by Christians (particularly Roman Catholics) on 25 March, it is often linked with the celebrations of Advent and Christmas. Many hymns and readings in churches during Advent include the Annunciation. It celebrates the visit of the Angel Gabriel to Mary to tell her that she had been chosen to have a child who would be the Son of God.

Discussion

Begin with a painting of the Annunciation such as the one painted by Leonardo da Vinci. Tell the children that the woman on the right-hand side is Mary and that the angel is telling her that she is going to have a baby who will be the Son of God.

Ask the children to look carefully at Mary. How can we tell that she is special? (The children may not notice the faint halo at first.) What is she like? Draw their attention to what she is doing and what sort of person she is. Who is giving her the news that she is going to have a special baby? (Draw attention to the angel's wings and halo.) How does Mary feel when she sees the angel? Point out the position of her left hand - it is raised, as if she is startled.

Other famous works of art showing the Annunciation are: *Adoration of the Magi* by Lorenzo Monaco; *Adoration of the Magi* by Gentile da Fabriano; *Madonna and Child* by Masaccio; *Nativity* by the Master of Flémalle; *Madonna Adoring Child* by Fra Filippo Lippi; *Nativity* by Piero della Francesca; and *St Columba Altarpiece* by Rogier van der Weyden.

Concept

In Christianity, the preparation for the birth of Jesus, beginning with the Annunciation

Activities

Provide hymn books so that the children can find hymns about the Annunciation, using the contents page and index. Ask them to notice any words that are common to several of the hymns. Why do they think these words are used so often? The children could find out about the Annunciation from works of art, hymns, prayers and the Bible (or a children's Bible) and then plan and act out the story.

The children could do their own 'Annunciation' paintings of Mary and the angel, in the style of Leonardo da Vinci or another artist. They could write about what is happening in the painting.

The children could make 'pleated' angels:

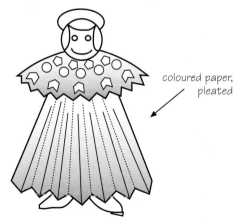

coloured paper, pleated

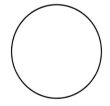

1 Cut a circle for the collar

2 Fold and fold again

3 **a** Cut a 'neck'
b Draw and cut out a lace pattern

4 Open out

The angel said to Mary, "Do not be afraid. The Lord has chosen you to bear His son."

Sam

Lois

Sophie

Stephen

Kirsty

Collette

Display

The children's 'Annunciation' paintings were framed with gold paper and mounted on a blue background, which is the colour often associated with Mary. The blue also suggests the sky, across which a banner bearing the words of the Angel Gabriel is unfurled.

Resources

A reproduction of a painting of the Annunciation; blue backing paper; white cartridge paper; paints and brushes; thin, brightly-coloured card or stiff paper; gold paper; hymn books; The Alternative Service Book; a Bible

Divali

Concepts

The symbolism of light; the celebration of an event of religious significance

Story

Read the story of Rama and Sita, which can be found in the *Ramayana* and in *Stanley Thornes Infant RE, Book Y2/P3*.

Explain that Divali is a Hindu (and Sikh) festival. If there are Hindu (or Sikh) children in the class, they could describe how they celebrate Divali.

Background

Divali is celebrated during the Hindu months of *Aashvin* and *Kartik* (approximately September and October). 'Divali' means a row of lights. The festival commemorates the story of Rama and Sita. Like many Hindu stories, its theme is the struggle between good and evil.

During Divali, Hindu temples and homes are decorated with candles and *divas* (lamps filled with *ghee* or clarified butter). Special foods are eaten, people exchange cards and gifts, and there are parties and fireworks.

Activities

Put some clarified butter or vegetable oil in each *diva* and place a wick or small piece of string in the oil with part of it protruding above the oil. Explain that when the wicks are lit the lamps will burn. If school guidelines permit, light the lamps. Talk about the welcoming feel of lights at night.

Talk about the kinds of things people do during any celebration such as wearing new clothes, eating special foods, preparing for the celebration, buying presents, sending cards, having a party, dancing, singing, or decorating their homes.

Read poems about celebrations, e.g. 'Funny Folk' by Robert Fisher, 'Corroboree' by Kath Walker, and 'Marty's Party' by David McCord, from the book *Welcome to the Party* (BBC 1993). Talk about how the poets make their poems sound joyful, like a celebration. The children could try to mimic the lively rhythm of these when they write their own 'party' poems.

Ask the children to paint pictures of lights at night. The pictures need not be realistic - just impressions of bright spots of light on a dark background.

Resources

Red backing paper; card; scraps of fabric; felt-tipped pens; scissors; a large piece of thin white fabric

Displays

In the display shown on page 38, the children dressed dolls to look like Rama and Sita. They glued the stories they had written on to 'book' shapes and displayed their *rangoli* patterns alongside. (*Rangoli* patterns are traditionally made from coloured ground rice.) Red was chosen for the background as it is the colour of happiness and good fortune in Hinduism.

The children also made shadow puppets and a screen to retell the story of Rama and Sita (see left).

Christmas

Discussion

Read about the events leading up to the birth of Jesus and the journeys of the people who visited him (Luke 1: 26-38, 46-55, 2: 1-20 and Matthew 1: 18-25, 2). Ask the children why Herod was afraid when he heard about the birth of Jesus (Matthew 2: 7-18). (He thought Jesus was going to be a warrior-king who would lead a great army against him.) Read the prophecy of the coming of Jesus (Isaiah 7: 13-16) and ask the children what the prophet was saying about the Messiah. (Christians believe that Jesus was born to save people from their sins, by dying.)

Display

The background was made from plain backing paper and Christmas wrapping paper (see right). In groups, the children sorted Christmas cards with religious, secular and traditional images into sets that show how people think of Christmas.

Concepts

The significance of the birth of Jesus to the early Christians and to the rulers of the land where he was born; the importance of the birth of Jesus to present-day Christians; the secular celebration of Christmas

Activities

Show the children triptychs of the Nativity (works of art that are in three sections with the centre panel showing the Nativity). The side panels can be closed to cover the centre panel and usually have some decoration on their reverse. The children could paint their own triptychs (see left), making sure they decorate the reverse of the side panels.

A chart could be made, where the children record some of the symbols used on Christmas cards. The children could research and try to explain the symbols.

Resources

A wide selection of Christmas cards; white card; white cartridge paper; Christmas wrapping paper; paints

Lent

Lent

Shrove Tuesday is the day before Lent begins

Pancakes

Ingredients
250g flour
a pinch of salt
1 egg
250ml milk

Method
Sieve flour and salt
Beat together egg and milk.
Stir into dry ingredients
Pour a cupful into greased frying pan. Cook until golden.

Christians try to give up a luxury

Luxuries

Necessities

sweets
television
football
ice cream

Given up

Concepts

Celebration of events of religious significance; symbolism; the distinction between luxuries/necessities and 'worldly'/'spiritual' concerns

Background

Lent is the forty-day period that precedes Easter. It begins on Ash Wednesday (in February or March) and commemorates the forty days in which, according to the Bible, Jesus was tempted by the devil in the wilderness (Matthew 4: 1-11, Luke 4: 1-13).

Discussion

Tell the children the story of Jesus in the wilderness. What do they think 'wilderness' means? Why did Jesus go there? Show them pictures of natural environments that few people visit. Could people be close to God in those places? Ask them to explain their answers.

Have the children heard people say they are giving something up for Lent? What sort of things are given up during Lent? (Luxuries)

Activities

Ask the children to close their eyes and imagine what a wilderness might look like. They could paint a picture of it and describe it.

Ask the children to choose something they will do without for forty days. How could this help other people? (If the children give up sweets, they could collect the money they would have spent and donate it to a local charity.)

Some children might be able to understand the difference between 'worldly' and 'spiritual' things. Begin by talking about things that can and cannot be bought, and then make a list.

Display

The display provides some information about Lent. The recipe is for pancakes, which are traditionally made on the day before Lent begins to use up rich foods in preparation for the fast. The children sorted a collection of pictures into 'luxuries' and 'necessities'. The heading and some of the lettering were cut from patterned gift-wrapping paper.

Resources

Reference material about Lent; yellow backing paper; patterned gift-wrapping paper; pictures of objects for sorting; pancake recipe

Easter

Concepts

The significance of the Easter story; Easter symbolism - new life; the resurrection of Jesus

Discussion

What do the children know about Easter? What symbols or pictures do they think of in connection with Easter? Do the children know any Easter songs or hymns? Record their responses on a large sheet of paper (this could be kept and referred to later, to assess what the children have learnt).

Give a crucifix to a small group of children. Ask them to describe it. Do they know whom it represents? What do they know about his death? Tell them that Jesus was a real person who was born nearly 2,000 years ago. The Christian calendar, which is now adopted as the universal calendar, began from the date of his birth.

Story

Read the story of the Crucifixion (Matthew 26-28; Luke 22-24).

After reading the story, describe what Christians believe about the Crucifixion, with reference to the Nicene Creed:
'We believe in one Lord, Jesus Christ, the only son of God...
...for our sake He was crucified under Pontius Pilate; He suffered death and was buried.
On the third day He rose again...
He ascended into Heaven and is seated at the right hand of the Father.'

Show the children works of art of the Crucifixion, and ask them to look for the characters from the story. Ask the children to describe the feelings of the people in the pictures. In some pictures, they should be able to find a feeling of hope as well as sorrow.

Activities

Make a collection of Easter cards and ask the children to list the symbols or pictures that appear on them. They could make a graph to show the occurrence of particular symbols in a given number of Easter cards.

Ask the children to look for symbols of new life on the Easter cards such as lambs, eggs, spring flowers and chicks. Can they explain why these symbols are associated with Easter? Explain that when Christianity was first introduced into Britain there were pagan spring festivals there already, whose symbols became associated with Easter.

The children could retell the story of the Crucifixion from the point of view of one of the disciples (including Judas), one of the chief priests, Jesus himself, or Pontius Pilate. Ask them to consider how their chosen character might have felt about the events and to research the story using a Bible, or a children's Bible, depending on their age and ability.

Resources

Works of art showing the Crucifixion; a crucifix; a collection of different kinds of Easter cards featuring flowers, chicks, lambs, and crucifixes; a Bible or children's Bible; *The Alternative Service Book* (HarperCollins Religious/CUP 1980)

On the Sunday morning

Whose tomb was it?

Why was it empty?

What did the angel say?

Who were the three women?

they came to the tomb.

Display

The display presents an image of the resurrection of Jesus. It includes a poster from *Stanley Thornes Infant RE, Book Y1/P2,* which features the painting *The Maries at the Sepulchre* by Andrea Mantegna. The questions stimulated the children's thinking about the Easter story.

Hanukkah

Background

Hanukkah is celebrated for eight days beginning between 25 *Kislev* - 2 *Tevet* (the third and fourth months of the Jewish calendar), which correspond approximately with

Concepts

Celebration of events of religious significance; symbolism

December. It commemorates the defeat of the Greeks by Judas Maccabaeus and his followers, who cleansed and rededicated the Temple. The Temple is deeply significant to Jews. Jewish scriptures and prayers contain references to the many occasions on which their enemies destroyed the Temple; each time the Jews rebuilt it.

Story

Read the story of Hanukkah to the children from *Stanley Thornes Infant RE, Book Y2/P3.* Explain that today every synagogue, like the Temple, has a light which is never allowed to go out. Nowadays these are usually electric lights.

Discussion

Ask the children if they can explain why the *hanukiah* (the special candle-holder used during the festival) has eight candles, plus an extra one (the *shammash* or servant) in the middle. Show them how the *shammash* is used to light one candle on each day of Hanukkah. Can the children explain why Hanukkah lasts for eight days?

Talk about the build-up of the festival feeling as a new candle is lit each day. How do the children feel when they prepare for a festival or other important event? What do they do to mark the time of waiting? Do they mark off days on a calendar or in a diary? Do they have a countdown of the days, even the hours, to the special day?

Talk about festivals that the children celebrate. They might be familiar with the celebration, but sometimes the meaning of a festival has been forgotten - it becomes simply a time for eating special foods and exchanging cards and gifts.

Activities

The children could make a large outline of the *hanukiah* from gold paper. They could cut out and glue on to it a flame each day for eight days (not forgetting to add the *shammash* candle).

Display

The children made gift containers and filled them with sweets and dried fruit. This was based on the *dreidls* used during a traditional Hanukkah game.

Many Jewish children play the *dreidl* game at Hanukkah. A handful of raisins, nuts or small sweets is needed, and a home-made spinner or plastic spinning top bearing the Hebrew letters *nun, gimmel, hey* and *shin*. (These are the initial letters of the Hebrew for 'a great miracle happened here'.)

nun   gimmel   hey   shin

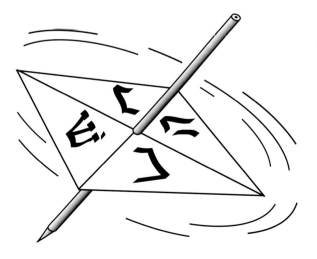

A dreidl

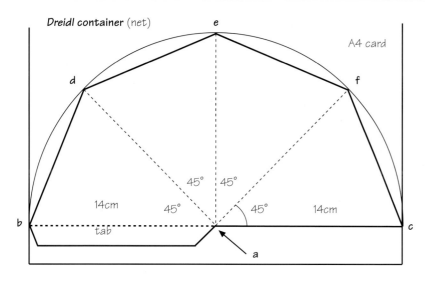

Dreidl container (net)

A4 card

e

d   f

45° 45°

14cm   45°   45°   14cm

b
tab

a

1 Draw line **bc** 28cm long

2 Draw a semi-circle (radius 14cm) with **a** as its centre

3 Use a protractor to measure 45° angles

4 Draw and score the lines **ad**, **ae**, **af**

5 Score line **ab** and add a tab

6 Write one of the Hebrew letters on each face of the container and decorate

7 Fold and glue the tab

The *dreidl* game

In the game the children follow these instructions, depending on which letter the spinner lands:

nun - do nothing;

gimmel - take all the raisins, nuts or sweets from the central pile;

hey - take half the pile of nuts, raisins or sweets;

shin - put all your nuts, raisins or sweets back on the pile.

Set a timer to signify the end of the game.

Resources

Card; scissors; coloured paper; glue; raisins and sweets; a manufactured *dreidl* or a home-made spinner

45

Wesak

Background

Wesak is the celebration of the birth, enlightenment and death of the Buddha some 2,500 years ago. Buddhists believe that all three events happened on the same day of different years. The festival takes place on the day of the full moon of the month of *Vishaka* (usually in May or June). It is a time when many Buddhists reflect on the past year and on their good and bad deeds. They might make resolutions for the following year; they meditate, trying to think only good thoughts; and they give presents or send money to people in need.

Buddhists celebrate Wesak in different ways. In Japan they wash statues of the Buddha with scented water. In Sri Lanka they decorate their homes and streets with lanterns. In Thailand they clean their homes and statues of the Buddha, hang up flags, streamers and garlands of flowers, and take part in candle-lit processions, sometimes with decorated elephants.

Discussion

Introduce the children to sayings that include the word 'light' such as 'he saw the light', 'there was light at the end of the tunnel' and 'to throw light on'. Use the sayings in contexts that help the children to work out the meaning. They should notice that light is often used to mean understanding or enlightenment as well as enabling people to see.

Explain how Buddhists think about their deeds of the past year. Ask the children to sit very quietly and to think of things they have done in the past year, and the effects these might have had on others. How will this affect the children's future actions?

Resources

Reference books about the Buddha; stories of the Buddha; white card; scissors; saffron and maroon backing paper; art paper

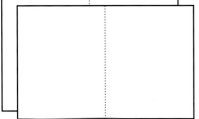

1 Take two pieces of A5 card

2 Fold one piece

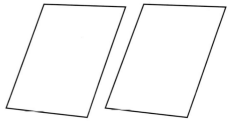

3 Cut the other piece in half to make two

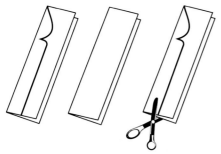

4 Fold the two smaller pieces and draw half a candle on one

5 Put the two pieces on top of each other and cut out the candle

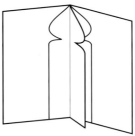

6 Glue the candles inside the card from 2

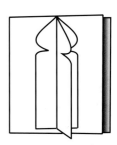

7 To make a candle for the front of the card, repeat 3 - 5

Colour and decorate the candles

Activities

The children could think about significant events in their own lives. Then they could look at memorable events that have taken place in their class or school. How could they commemorate this event each year? They could plan a celebration. Ask them how they might prepare for it - perhaps by making decorations and costumes, preparing special food, and having a procession.

Tell the children what the Buddha told his followers to do: to stop people suffering in any way and to try to have 'good' thoughts, whatever others may do. Ask the children to draw and label some of the things that make people suffer - being poor or sick, being hurt by others' unkind words and deeds, or when people they love die. The children could think of ways in which they could help to stop the suffering of others. They could raise money to help a local charity, after finding out about its work.

The children could make Wesak greetings cards, using symbols of light such as candles and specifically Buddhist symbols such as the lotus flower. They could make pop-up candle cards (see above).

Concepts

The use of light as a symbol for enlightenment; celebrating the life of a key figure of a faith; the effects of our actions, words, and even thoughts, on others

Display

The children used library books to find out about the important events in the life of the Buddha. They made paper lanterns and decorated them. A background of saffron and maroon was used, as these are the colours of the robes of Tibetan Buddhist monks.

Ramadan and Id-ul-Fitr

Background

Ramadan is a time of prayer and fasting for devout Muslims, who neither eat nor drink during daylight hours. At the end of Ramadan is Id-ul-Fitr, a happy festival that celebrates the glory of Allah (God) and each individual's achievement of fasting. The dates of Ramadan and Id-ul-Fitr move forward each year because of the Islamic lunar calendar.

Discussion

Explain that fasting shows Muslims are not thinking of themselves nor of everyday things, but of God. Ask the children what it must be like to fast. How do they think Muslims feel towards the end of each fasting day? How might they feel as Id-ul-Fitr approaches? Talk about events that the children have looked forward to, how they felt and how they prepared for them.

Activities

Provide dates and water for the children to eat and drink, as Muslims do to end each day's fast during Ramadan.

Buy Id-ul-Fitr greetings cards from mosques, educational suppliers or shops in areas with a Muslim population. Talk about the designs and calligraphy and help the children to design their own cards. The cards should not depict people or animals, as this is strictly forbidden by the Qur'an as making idols.

Display

The children drew 'clock' charts to show a typical day in the life of a Muslim over the age of ten during Ramadan. They painted 'light' and 'dark' pictures. The display background is in the dark blue associated with Islam. The prayer mats are a reminder that Ramadan is a time for prayer as well as fasting.

Concepts

Fasting and feasting in religious festivals; devotion

Resources

Dark blue backing paper; prayer mat; reference material about Ramadan

Special people

Discussion

Ask the children to name someone they think is special. What makes these people special? Introduce the idea that there is something about everyone which makes them special. Invite the children to say what is special about themselves and other members of the class.

Display

Using magazines, newspapers and catalogues, the children cut out pictures of faces, which they arranged as a collage on a background of white paper. This was cut out, leaving a small border, and mounted on red paper. The border, small pictures and lettering were cut from a wallpaper border with a bright, cheerful pattern in red, white and yellow. The lettering can either be traced on to the patterned paper by using stencils or drawn lightly in pencil before cutting out. Red and yellow were chosen to give a cheerful, welcoming effect.

Activities

The children could paint portraits of their own 'special people'. These could be members of their family, friends or people in the community. Below each picture the children could copy and complete the sentence: '... is special because ...'

Display the portraits on a wallpaper background paper chosen to give the effect of a picture frame. The children's paintings can each be trimmed and framed in a different 'picture frame' wallpaper.

The children could contribute to a poster entitled 'A good friend is a special person'. With an adult acting as scribe, they could give examples of things that good friends do. They could add a border to the poster, made up of drawings of their friends.

Concept

Characteristics that make everyone special

Resources

Red and white backing paper; wallpaper border with a bright pattern; newspapers, magazines and catalogues

Discussion

Ask the children to name some saints. Where have they heard or seen their names, and what do they know about them? The children might know

the names of saints associated with local churches, schools or place names, patron saints of countries or groups of people, or saints associated with particular days of the year, such as St Valentine.

If possible, provide works of art showing events from the lives of saints. What can the children find out about the saints from them? Useful paintings and sculptures include:
St Francis and the Birds by Stanley Spencer (Tate Gallery, London);
St John the Baptist and St Matthew by Lorenzo Ghiberti (Orsanmichele, Florence);
St George Slaying the Dragon by Donatello (Orsanmichele, Florence);
St Joseph by The Master of Flémalle from the *Mérode Altarpiece* (Metropolitan Museum of Art, New York);
The Life of St Francis by Sassetta (National Gallery, London);
St Michael by Bartolomé Bermejo (Luton Hoo, Bedfordshire);
The Four Apostles by Albrecht Dürer (Alte Pinakothek, Munich).

Make a collection of pictures of stained glass windows and postcards depicting saints. These can often be bought from art gallery and cathedral shops (or ordered from them by telephone).

Display

The children made 'stained glass window' pictures of their chosen saints. The pictures include symbols that tell about the saint, e.g. a wheel was shown with St Catherine of Alexandria because she was burned to death while strapped on a wheel. The 'stained glass windows' were attached to the windows using double-sided Sellotape. This can be removed later with surgical spirit.

Activities

Provide guide books about the local area and ask the children to look for places that have been named after saints. They could draw and label these places, perhaps incorporating photographs or sketches of signs bearing the saints' names. If possible, make a display of photographs of signs showing place names that are saints' names.

Provide reference books on saints such as *A Concise Dictionary of Saints*, *Signs and Symbols* by W Ellwood Post (SPCK). The children could find out about the saints featured in local place names. Are there any symbols or signs associated with the saints? Where and when did they live? Are there any miracles associated with them? What are their life stories? Local churches may be able to supply information about their own saints, and cathedrals often have booklets about the saints associated with them. The children could write 'pen pictures' or compile fact files about these saints.

Resources

Reference books about saints; local guide books; works of art on posters, postcards or books showing saints; coloured acetate; black paper; double-sided adhesive tape

Jesus

Concepts

Key people in religions; the significance of Jesus to Christians; the character of Jesus

Story

A crowd of people thronged around Jesus and his disciples; the people had listened to Jesus for many hours and were still questioning him about the things he had taught them. But it was time to rest. Jesus asked his disciples to take him out to the middle of the lake where they could find peace to pray and prepare for the next day's teaching.

Before long Jesus was asleep, but the others were worried that the dark clouds gathering in the sky were bringing a storm. The wind grew stronger and the waves slapped against the boat. And Jesus slept on. The others became more and more anxious as the boat lurched and the water crashed over its sides. And Jesus slept on.

'Lord, save us!' they cried in terror. Jesus opened his eyes and slowly sat up. He looked at the waves and said, 'Be quiet.' He looked at the wind and said, 'Peace, be still.' The wind dropped and the waves lapped gently, and Jesus said to his disciples, 'You should not have been afraid. Where was your faith?'

His friends had lost their fear. Now they looked at each other in astonishment, saying, 'Who is this man? Even the winds and waves obey him.'

Discussion

Allow the children a few minutes to reflect on the story. Then ask them to talk to a partner about what the story tells them about Jesus. What had he been doing, and what did the people think of his teaching? How was Jesus different from ordinary people? What was he trying to teach his friends by stopping the storm?

Activities

The children could read more stories about Jesus, looking for events that show his teaching, healing, miracles and his love for all people, even those whom nobody else seemed to love. Examples include:

Teaching
The Sermon on the Mount (Matthew 5: 1-16); the Parable of the Sower (Matthew 3: 3-8); the Lord's Prayer (Matthew 6: 7-18); the Beatitudes (Luke 6: 20-49).

Healing
Jairus and his daughter (Mark 9: 18-26); the woman who had been bent double for eighteen years (Luke 13: 10-17); the man with the withered arm (Luke 6: 6-11); the blind beggar (Luke 18: 35-43).

Miracles
The Raising of Lazarus (Luke 16: 19-31); the Wedding at Cana (John 2: 1-11); the Feeding of the Five Thousand (John 6: 1-14).

Love
Eating with tax-collectors and sinners (Luke 15: 1-7); Jesus blessing the children (Matthew 18: 1-14); and all the stories of Jesus healing sick and disabled people.

In groups, ask the children to choose one of these stories and turn it into a short play that they could present to the rest of the class or even to the whole school, perhaps during collective worship.

Resources

An atlas or map of Israel and its surrounding countries; a word-processor

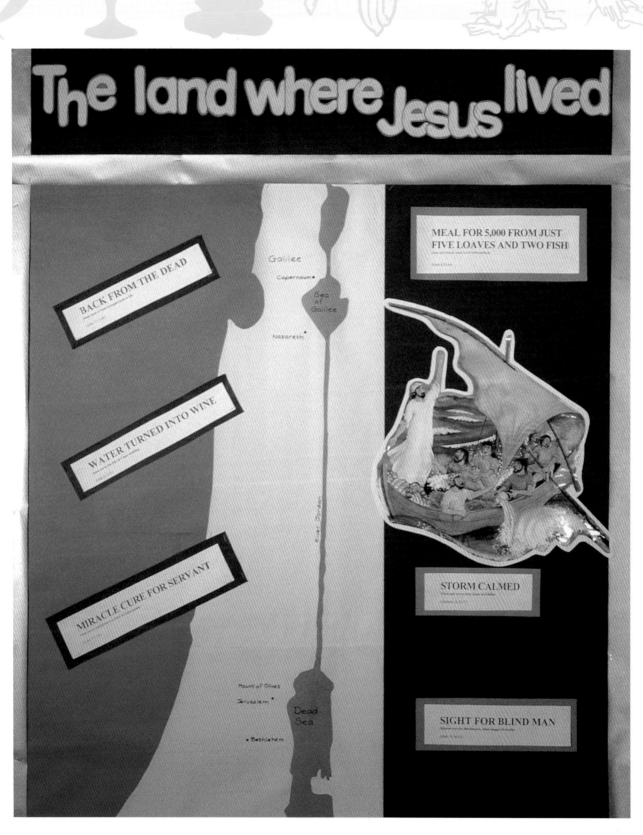

The land where Jesus lived

BACK FROM THE DEAD

WATER TURNED INTO WINE

MIRACLE CURE FOR SERVANT

MEAL FOR 5,000 FROM JUST FIVE LOAVES AND TWO FISH

STORM CALMED

SIGHT FOR BLIND MAN

Galilee
Capernaum
Sea of Galilee
Nazareth
River Jordan
Mount of Olives
Jerusalem
Dead Sea
Bethlehem

Display

The children copied and enlarged a map of Israel and its neighbouring countries. Then they fixed word-processed 'headlines' to show where some of the stories they had researched took place.

Muhammad (pbuh)

Background

The names of the prophets of Islam are always followed by 'peace be upon him', or Islamic calligraphy that means this. These words are shortened to 'pbuh', or 'pbut' if more than one prophet is named. Explain to the children that Muslims do this as a sign of respect. Muslims revere Muhammad (pbuh) as the founder of the faith and God's messenger.

Concepts

Prophets; the importance of Muhammad (pbuh) to Muslims

Resources

Magazines, postcards and travel brochures; pictures of places (rural and urban); a copy of the Qur'an; examples of Islamic calligraphy

Story

Muhammad was born in about 570CE in Makkah (Mecca), which is in the country now known as Saudi Arabia. He married Khadijah and they had six children. People respected Muhammad because he was honest in business. In the evenings he would go to a cave on Mount Hira near Makkah to pray. The cave is now revered as a holy place.

One evening an angel appeared to Muhammad and said that he would tell him the words of God and that Muhammad must remember every word. The angel's words are the words of the Qur'an, the holy book of Islam. The Qur'an tells stories of the prophets and gives instructions about how Allah (God) wanted people to live. Muhammad told his family and friends what the angel had said. They all learned the words by heart and after Muhammad died his followers wrote them down.

Another night an angel took Muhammad into the heavens, saying, 'Look out for a caravan of camels that is going to arrive in Makkah; leading it will be a camel carrying a double load - half wrapped in a black cloth and half wrapped in a cloth of many colours.'

Muhammad wanted to teach the people of Makkah about Allah's wishes. He saw people worshipping idols and said that Allah forbade this. Some people listened to him but most did not. He was forced to leave Makkah. Then Muhammad saw the camel carrying the load the angel had described.

When he saw this sign Muhammad decided to go to Madinah (Medina) to see if the people there would listen to him. His family and friends went with him. This journey is remembered as *Hijrah*, which means 'emigration'. The year was 622CE. The people in Madinah listened to what Muhammad said and the Islamic calendar began on this date, the first of the month of *Muharram.*

In 632CE the Muslims went back and captured Makkah. There Muhammad helped to rebuild the Ka'bah, the first place of worship for Muslims. The first man, Adam (pbuh), had built the very first Ka'bah but it had fallen into ruin. It is now the most holy Muslim building. Muslims from all over the world visit it every year for the Hajj (pilgrimage). At other times, wherever they are when they pray, Muslims turn to face the direction of the Ka'bah.

Discussion

Ask the children why Muhammad chose a cave in the mountains as a place to pray. Where would they choose to go to be alone with God?

Can the children imagine what an angel looks like, does and says? Do they think angels really exist? Where? To whom do angels talk, and why?

Muhammad (pbuh) is special to Muslims

Born in Makkah	570
Married Khadijah.	
An angel spoke to him on Mount Hira	
The Qur'an was revealed.	
The Night Journey	
The Hijra (in Madinah)	622
Returned to Makkah	630
Died in Madinah.	632

Activities

Provide magazines, postcards and travel brochures so that the children can cut out pictures of places where people could go to be close to God. How do the children think people feel when they are close to God? The children could talk about why they have chosen a particular place, and then write about it.

Display

The children made a timeline to show the main events in the life of the Prophet, who is not depicted as this is not allowed in Islam.

Moses

Concept

The significance of Moses to Jews

Story

Read to the children the story of how Moses was found as a baby among the bulrushes on the River Nile by the Pharaoh's daughter (Exodus 2: 1-10).

Discussion

Ask the children to describe the feelings of Hebrew mothers. How do the children think the king's officials felt about their job of hunting out and killing baby boys? The children should recognise that there would be a mixture of feelings. The officials were Egyptian and they thought of the Hebrews as a danger to the state.

Activities

Ask the children to imagine they are investigative journalists pursuing a rumour that a Hebrew baby boy has been kept hidden from the king's officials. The children have to write a report for their newspaper. They could give the paper a name, using names of places or words mentioned in the Bible such as *The Nile Times*, *The Desert Star* or *The Egypt Herald*.

Display

The blue background represents the river. The basket was cut from thin straw matting. Real bulrushes (from a florist) were stapled on to the display board and the border was cut from newspaper.

Resources

Blue backing paper; newspaper; word-processing software that can create a 'newspaper format'; straw matting; bulrushes; Bible

Guru Nanak

Concepts

Founders of religions; communicating with God

Background

Nanak (1469-1539CE) was born in the part of the Indian sub-continent now called Pakistan, in a well-to-do family. From an early age he was interested in religion, and by the time he was thirty he was meditating regularly about God and composing hymns and psalms. His joyful yet quiet and peaceful way of worshipping attracted many followers, called Sikhs (disciples), who gathered regularly to join him in singing his psalms and hymns. Many of these songs became part of the Guru Granth Sahib, the Sikh holy book. Nanak became known as Guru Nanak, the first of the ten Sikh Gurus.

Story

Read the story of Guru Nanak from *Stanley Thornes Infant RE, Book Y2/P3.*

Display

Around a poster of Guru Nanak are displayed the children's descriptions of what made him special. (The poster is from *Folens Religious Education, Age 5-7.*) Also displayed are the children's own paintings of Guru Nanak.

Activities

The children could look at a poster of Guru Nanak and describe how they can tell he is special. Draw their attention to the position in which he is sitting, the halo around his head, and his calm, peaceful expression. What sort of person do they think he is?

The children could talk about and describe what made other people listen to Guru Nanak and want to worship with him.

Resources

Blue and gold fabric; a picture of Guru Nanak

The Buddha

Concepts

Founders of religions; authority; lifestyle

Background

'The Buddha' means 'the enlightened one'. The Buddha (Siddattha Gotama: 563-483 BCE), who lived in northern India, was enlightened (came to understand the meaning of life) while sitting meditating beneath a *bodhi* tree.

Story

Prince Siddattha Gotama was born nearly 2,600 years ago in Lumbini, Nepal. At his naming ceremony, it was predicted that he would become either a great king or a religious teacher. To make sure he grew up to be a good man, his father kept him in the royal palace away from all the evil things in the world. Siddattha grew up, got married and had children, without leaving the palace grounds.

Then Siddattha decided to see the world. He set off with his servant. Soon they saw an old man leaning on a stick, hardly able to walk. 'What is wrong with him?' asked Siddattha, who had never seen any old people. The servant replied, 'He is suffering because his body is worn out. It happens to everyone who lives to a great age.'

Further on there was what looked like a bundle of rags lying at the side of the road. Then the bundle moved and groaned. Siddattha queried his servant, who replied, 'She is suffering because she is ill.'

Next they came upon a group of people surrounding a great pile of sandalwood. There was a body on top of the pile, wrapped in a cloth. Someone lit the wood. 'Death, and suffering,' said the servant.

Siddattha saw a very thin man sitting cross-legged on a mat. He was naked except for a cloth wrapped around the lower part of his body. 'He is a holy man,' said the servant. 'He spends his time thinking about the meaning of life. He eats just enough to keep himself alive.'

Resources

A statuette or picture of the Buddha; mandalas; maroon and gold backing paper; gold fabric

'There has to be an answer to all this suffering,' thought Siddattha. He travelled all over India looking for the answer. 'I need to find a middle way,' he thought. 'The middle way will be somewhere between starving like the holy men and living like a prince, as I once did.'

Eventually Siddattha went back to Nepal. There he sat beneath a *bodhi* tree and thought deeply about life. These are the answers he found - the Four Noble Truths of Buddhism:
'All life has suffering.
Suffering comes from people wanting things.
Suffering stops when people stop wanting things.
Follow the Middle Way.'

Discussion

Show the children a statuette or poster of the Buddha and ask them to describe him, drawing their attention to his sitting position, his clothing, his hands, head and face (particularly the eyes). How can the children tell he was a holy man?

Give the children time to look quietly at the Buddha and ask them what they think he is doing. They might think he is praying, meditating or thinking. How can they tell? Ask the children to list the feelings that are suggested by the statue such as calmness, peacefulness, and holiness.

Activities

The children could try meditating. Show them pictures of *mandalas* (circular patterns), on which many Buddhists focus their attention while meditating. The children could make their own *mandalas* and could concentrate on them while thinking 'good thoughts'. Afterwards ask the children about their good thoughts. How could these thoughts make their school a happier place?

Display

The children's *mandalas,* drawn and coloured using felt-tipped pens, are displayed next to papers on which they have written some of their 'good thoughts'. The papers are shown blowing away in a breeze, since Buddhist belief is that the world can be changed by good thoughts (as well as good deeds) as these thoughts become part of existence. The poster is from *Stanley Thornes Infant RE, Book Y2/P3.*

The church

Concepts

The special design of churches for Christian worship; symbols

Discussion

Before a church visit

Make sure that the person who will show the children around the church knows they are going to look at the things that show it is a Christian church such as symbols, the direction it faces, pictures, windows, statues, and the way its design helps people to worship. Check whether the children will be allowed to make rubbings and take photographs.

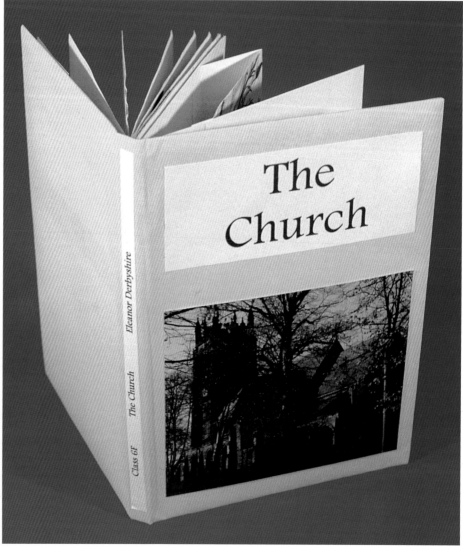

Prepare the children for their visit. Explain that they are going to look at the building and its contents to find out how a church is different and how that difference helps people to worship. The children will also look for things that are used in special ceremonies such as baptisms, holy communion, weddings and funerals. They will need to make notes and do drawings and, if possible, take photographs and make rubbings.

Using reference books and photographs, help the children to list the names of different parts of a church and its contents such as nave, transept, altar, pew, hassock, hymn board, lectern, font.

After the visit

Ask the children to name some of the things that make the church different from other buildings. Why does it have these things? How do they help people to worship? How are they used? The children could describe the symbols they found in the church.

Resources

Books about churches; compasses; clip-boards; pencils; camera(s); white (A4) paper; art paper; wax crayons; stiff card; decorated paper (such as gift-wrapping); felt-tipped pens; scissors; glue

The graveyard

The oldest graves are from the eighteenth century. The headstones are made of different kinds of stone. The oldest ones are made of sandstone which was quarried at Woolton Quarry in Liverpool. They have become grey or black and the lettering is wearing away. It is rounded - not sharp like the lettering on the new headstones.

The new headstones are made of marble: pink, white and black. The lettering on most of these is black. On the headstones it tells the name of the person, when they were born, when they died and how old they were when they died. On some it says "In loving memory" and on others "Sadly missed".

In Loving Memory

Activities

During the visit

Take some compasses (one for each group of five or six children) and ask the children to find out the directions the nave and transept of the church face. Ask the children to find the special parts of the church that were discussed before the visit and then draw, photograph or make rubbings of them, as appropriate. Different groups of children could focus on different parts of the church.

After the visit

Ask the children to use their notes from the visit to write about the part of the church they looked at in detail - what it is made of, its purpose, how it is used, what it looks like.

Display

The children made books about their local churches to show how different parts of the church - pews, the font, the altar, hymn boards, the pulpit, hassocks and a holy water stoop - are used in worship. They also included church decoration and symbols such as the cross, statues, stained glass, embroidery, tapestry, paintings and carvings. Some pages featured two-dimensional pictures, some incorporated three-dimensional 'pop-up' pictures, and some had text with decorative borders using motifs observed in the church.

The home shrine

Background

The numerous gods and goddesses of Hinduism are part of the Supreme Being, Brahman (not to be confused with Brahma, the Creator). The other two main gods are Shiva (the Destroyer) and Vishnu (the Preserver). The main goddesses are Saraswati, the goddess of wisdom and learning; Lakshmi, the goddess of good fortune; and Durga, the warrior goddess.

Discussion

Show the children some *murtis* (pictures and statuettes of Hindu deities). Who are these people? Ask the children how they can tell that these are not ordinary people. Talk about the Hindu deities, explaining that Hindus worship one God, Brahman, but in many different forms - some male and some female. The *murtis* are there to help Hindus concentrate on worship, not to be worshipped themselves.

Concepts

The different sides to a person's character; the worship of God in diverse forms; symbols

Activities

The children could talk to a partner about different aspects of their own character and draw pictures that portray themselves in different ways.

Children could research the Hindu deities, compile fact-files about them and write about why people might address their prayers to a particular deity, e.g. someone starting a new business might pray to Lakshmi, the goddess of good fortune.

Display

Red was chosen for the background because in Hinduism it is an auspicious colour. Using paper, fabric, bead foil, buttons and ribbon, the children made collages of the deities. The collages show the colour traditionally used for the skin of each deity, the forehead markings, the correct number of arms and the symbols associated with him or her.

Resources

Pictures and reference material about Hindu deities; red backing paper; foil; coloured paper; fabric; ribbon and buttons

The gurdwara

The Nishan Sahib

A gurdwara always has a kitchen

A gurdwara is a Sikh temple. Some are converted buildings such as churches

They always have a special flag

Concepts

The place of the gurdwara in a Sikh community; sharing; equality

Discussion

Ask the children to think of buildings that have a special purpose. How can the children tell the purpose of a building? How can they tell which buildings are places of worship?

Activities

If possible, take the children to a gurdwara (Sikh temple). Provide pictures and reference material about gurdwaras and ask the children to draw and describe anything special they notice. How can they tell that a building is a gurdwara? Point out the *Nishan Sahib* (Sikh flag).

What is the gurdwara like inside? Point out the *langar* (kitchen), the Guru Granth Sahib (the holy book) resting on a cushion beneath a canopy, shoe racks and floor mats. The children could find out how Sikhs worship and how the features of the gurdwara are designed to help them worship: the kitchen is where a meal is cooked to be shared by all worshippers (Sikhs and non-Sikhs) to show that everyone is welcome; everyone sits on the floor to show that all people are equal before God; the holy book is treated as if it were a person (it is regarded as the living guru now that there are no more human gurus) and accorded great respect; and worshippers take off their shoes as they enter, as a sign of respect.

Resources

Pictures and reference material about gurdwaras; blue backing paper; Nishan Sahib (see page 80); rolled paper

Display

The display is for information. The blue background is the colour of the *Khanda*, the symbol of Sikhism, on the *Nishan Sahib*. The 'flagpole' is made from rolled paper. (The flag and poster were kindly loaned by TTS Religion in Evidence.)

The mosque

Discussion

If possible, take the children to visit a mosque. Alternatively, collect and display photographs, posters and reference books showing exteriors and interiors of mosques. Draw the children's attention to the design of the building - most mosques have domes, or dome shapes incorporated into their design, and a minaret, the tower from which the *adhan* (the Call to Prayer) is sounded by the *muadhin*. (In some mosques nowadays a recording of the *adhan* is played over a loudspeaker.)

The children will notice that there are no seats in the mosque. Can they explain this? It is because Muslims do not sit during prayer. Instead they have a series of different postures for each section. If the mosque is carpeted, the carpet is usually marked into small rectangular sections facing the *qiblah* wall (the wall that faces Makkah), since Muslims face Makkah when they pray. In uncarpeted mosques, worshippers are provided with prayer mats.

Show the children pictures of the interiors of Christian churches and Hindu temples. Ask them how the decoration of the mosque is different. They should notice the absence of any human or animal forms (these would be equivalent to idols, which are strictly forbidden in Islam). Draw attention to the flower shapes and Islamic calligraphy (the language of Islam is Arabic). The calligraphy usually consists of verses from the Qur'an.

Activities

Ask the children to design their own mosques, taking into account the shape of the building and its different parts, the shapes of the windows and alcoves and the decoration of the walls. Ask them to draw the inside as well as the outside. Some children might even be able to draw a plan, labelling the important parts of the building.

Display

An outline of a mosque was drawn over the whole display board. The children made decorative tiles by colouring the raised patterns on embossed white wallpaper and copying Arabic calligraphy and patterns on to hexagons of paper. These were then glued on to the outline. The children's tiles (see right) showed a range of different patterns, based on their observations of the walls of mosques.

65

A place to meditate

A Peaceful Place

feeling stressed   feeling calm

Concept

Quiet reflection

Discussion

Provide a selection of photographs, postcards and magazines, from which the children can find pictures of different places. Ask them to sort the images into places where they would find peace to think, and places where they would not. The children should work in groups, deciding what makes some places suitable for this purpose. Ask them to find a picture of a place where someone might go to be close to God. Why have they chosen this place?

Display

From their class's designs, the children chose the best idea for a place for quiet thought or reflection. On a background of sky-blue and grass-green backing paper they made a collage of it, using coloured paper and outlines of flowers cut from photographs.

Activities

The children could sort pictures of people into two groups: 'calm and peaceful' and 'not calm and peaceful'. How can they tell how someone feels? They could draw or paint one person from each group.

The children could design and make a place for quiet reflection in the classroom. In their groups, ask them to discuss and list the things this special place would need. How would they make and keep it quiet? What might give it a peaceful feel? What would help those who use it to be calm and thoughtful? What would be the most suitable colours?

Resources

Magazines, travel brochures, postcards and photographs of places; green and blue backing paper; coloured paper and tissue paper; photographs of flowers

Discussion

Ask the children about books that are special to them. They could explain to the rest of the class what makes their particular book special.
How do they look after it? When do they read it?

Concepts

Special books; books for particular purposes

Activities

Provide a collection of books for the children to sort. The children could devise their own categories and list the titles on a chart. They could make and bind their own 'special books', into which they could copy the best stories they have written (see below).

Help the children to make their own bookmarks bearing their initials in decorative lettering.

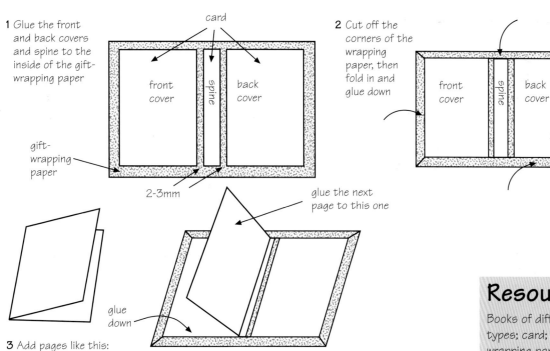

1 Glue the front and back covers and spine to the inside of the gift-wrapping paper

card

front cover   spine   back cover

gift-wrapping paper

2-3mm

2 Cut off the corners of the wrapping paper, then fold in and glue down

front cover   spine   back cover

glue the next page to this one

glue down

3 Add pages like this:

Resources

Books of different types; card; gift-wrapping paper; plain and lined paper; embroidery thread (for bookmark tassels); glue

Display

The children made their own special books with covers made from gift-wrapping paper, stiffened with card. They made bookmarks and 'illuminated' letters.

The Bibleௐ

Discussion

What do the children know about the Bible? Ask them what it is about, who reads it and why, and what sort of writings are in it.

Displays

The children copied their favourite proverbs, which were displayed in the form of 'open books' (see page 69). They wrote with felt-tipped pens and then glued their 'book' on to contrasting backing paper to form a bright border. The letters of the heading were drawn in a style that reminded the children of the illuminated letters found in old copies of the Bible.

Another display was made to look like a bookshelf (see above), showing the spines of books (the books of the Bible). The children cut out spines, whose widths reflected the number of pages in each book of the Bible (they calculated this by deciding on a number of 'pages per centimetre').

Concepts

The Bible as the book that guides the lives of Christians; the different kinds of writing in the Bible; proverbs as sayings to make people think about the results of their own actions; psalms as the poetry and songs of the Bible

Resources

Bibles; children's Bibles; reference books showing illuminated letters; felt-tipped pens; glue; purple backing paper and contrasting backing paper

Activities

Provide groups of children with a Bible or children's Bible and ask each group to read a specific section: one or two psalms; some proverbs; a parable; an historical account; and laws or rules. Examples include: Psalms 23, 121, 136, 137; Proverbs 10: 1-20; the Parable of the Lost Sheep (Matthew 18: 12-14), the Parable of the Labourers in the Vineyard (Matthew 20: 1-18), the Parable of the Talents (Matthew 25: 14-30); the Journey to the Promised Land (Exodus 16), the Nativity (Matthew 1: 18-25, 2: 1-17); the Rules of the Israelites (Leviticus 7: 22-27), the Ten Commandments (Exodus 20: 1-17).

Ask the children to which category the writings they have studied belong - poetry, wise sayings, stories that are accounts, stories with meanings, and laws and rules. They could write about the purposes of each type of writing, and about when and why Christians might read them, e.g. to praise God, to find out about the teachings of Jesus, or to learn or remind themselves of God's laws.

The children could copy some well-known proverbs and cut them in half for a partner to match.

The Guru Granth Sahib

Background

The Guru Granth Sahib (the holy book of Sikhism) is not kept in Sikh homes but only at a gurdwara (Sikh temple), where it is

Concepts

Holy books; respect for sacred texts

treated as a 'living guru' and accorded the respect due to a sacred text or to a guru. It consists of a collection of teachings of the first five gurus plus some writings of Hindus and Muslims, and was assembled by Guru Arjan Dev. It is written in ancient Punjabi, which few Sikhs today understand, yet it is the main source of guidance for the Sikh community.

Before use, the Guru Granth Sahib is placed on a special cushion under a canopy. Sikhs show respect by bowing to it. At night it is put away as if being put to bed, just like a living guru.

Some verses from the Guru Granth Sahib include:

> You are a tree;
> your beautiful branches are everywhere.
>
> Who made the stars which twinkle in the midnight sky?
> Who made the sun?
> Who made the moon?
> Whose light is all around me?
>
> Who makes the waves rise up from the sea?
> Who makes the seeds sprout and grow?
> Who ripens the fruit on the trees?
>
> You are very dear to me,
> as dear as milk is to a baby,
> as a flower is to a humming bee,
> as a pond is to a fish,
> as I need water on a hot day,
> I need you.

Discussion

Ask the children how they would look after a book that is very precious and must not be damaged in any way. How could they show other people the importance of the book? Help them to find out as much as possible about the Guru Granth Sahib, including why it is not easy to find it in bookshops or libraries.

Activities

Using reference books, the children could find translations of verses of the Guru Granth Sahib and copy some of them in their best writing. How could the children display these verses to show that they are holy and belong to the Sikh faith? How can they make them look special?

The verses could be printed out in suitable computer fonts and decorated with Sikh symbols and natural objects of beauty such as flowers.

Display

Gold was chosen for the background and dark blue for the lettering as these are colours often associated with Sikhism (the Sikh flag, the *Nishan Sahib,* is blue and gold). Some of the children's writing was copied and glued on to paper and then displayed to look like the pages of an open book on a cushion (see page 70). Words from the Guru Granth Sahib were copied using letter templates and glued across the display.

Resources

Reference books containing words from the Guru Granth Sahib; gold and blue backing paper; white paper; letter templates

The Qur'an

Concepts

Special books; teachings and rules for living

Background

The Qur'an is treated with great reverence. Before touching it, Muslims perform *wudu* (symbolic washing). During use the Qur'an is placed on a stand so that it is not touched unnecessarily.

Discussion

Display books that give instructions for particular occasions and situations such as books about etiquette for weddings, formal dinners and writing letters. Can the children think of places (e.g. sports centres, clubs) that have their own rules of etiquette?

Activities

The children could write their own instructions for living a 'good' life. They should describe the everyday things that people can do in order to be 'good people'. They could consider how they behave towards other people such as family members, classmates, teachers, people in authority and people less fortunate than themselves. Ask the children to compare their rules with some from the Qur'an.

Provide a collection of book stands for the children to examine such as cookery book stands, lecterns used for talks, and music stands. They should notice the way in which the design of each stand suits its purpose. Why are some stands and lecterns tall and some (including the Qur'an stand) short? The Qur'an stand is placed on the ground (usually on a carpet) and the reader sits on a cushion on the ground.

The children could design and make Qur'an stands:

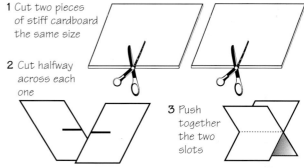

1 Cut two pieces of stiff cardboard the same size

2 Cut halfway across each one

3 Push together the two slots

Display

The children's 'rules for living' are displayed, together with parts of the Qur'an that they have copied and some of their attempts at Islamic calligraphy. Their Qur'an stand designs are also displayed. The blue background reflects one of the colours associated with Islam.

Resources

A copy of the Qur'an; card from cereal boxes; coloured paper; string; glue

Concepts

Rules; lifestyle

Discussion

Buddhists believe that the way to achieve enlightenment is to follow the Noble Eightfold Path (see below). Read the Noble Eightfold Path with the children and ask them what they think each precept means, and how people might behave if they were following it.

The Noble Eightfold Path of Buddhism

The Buddha

Right seeing
Right thought
Right action
Right speech
Right livelihood
Right effort
Right mindfulness
Right contemplation

1 Right intention
The intention of keeping to the Noble Eightfold Path and believing the Four Noble Truths (see page 59).

2 Right values
Behaving with kindness and love and rejecting selfishness and greed.

3 Right speech
Speaking well of people; avoiding lies and gossip.

4 Right behaviour
Overcoming bad thoughts with good and letting the good thoughts control behaviour.

5 Right living
Working to the best of your ability at an occupation that is in keeping with the Four Noble Truths.

6 Right effort
Learning to know yourself and to follow the Noble Eightfold Path in a way that suits you; avoiding evil; doing good deeds which bring you merit for a better rebirth.

7 Right mindedness
Being calm, and free from desires for unnecessary things.

8 Right contemplation
Learning how to control your mind so that it does not wander when you meditate on the meaning of life.

Resources

Reference material about the rules of Buddhism; maroon and yellow backing paper; letter templates

Activities

Eight groups could each discuss one precept from the Noble Eightfold Path. The children could enact a scene showing people who do and do not follow that rule. Ask them to draw picture stories, using speech and thought 'bubbles' to show these scenes. The picture stories should each fill a sheet of A3 paper, which will form part of the display.

Display

The children's stories are displayed with the colours associated with Tibetan Buddhist monks' robes.

Parables

Discussion

Before reading the stories

Talk about times when things are lost in the classroom. When the children tidy up at the end of a lesson, what happens if there is a pair of scissors or a book missing? What does the class think about most - the lost scissors or book, or the ones that are in their right places?

The children could describe times when they have lost something, the places they searched, how they felt, what they thought, said and did. Then, when they found whatever was lost, what did they think, say and do? How did they feel?

Stories

Read *The Lost Coin* (Luke 15: 8-10).
Then read *The Lost Sheep* (Luke 15: 3-6).

Ask the children to describe how these stories are similar - something was lost, someone looked for it, and there was great rejoicing when it was found. Draw the children's attention to the way in which the characters in the stories ignored their possessions that were not lost to give all their attention to finding the lost one.

Story

Read *The Lost Son* (Luke 15: 12-32).

Ask the children why the father ignored the hard-working son who stayed at home, and rejoiced when the other son came home, even though he had spent all his time and money on enjoying himself.

Tell the children about the occasion on which Jesus told these stories: he had spent a long time talking to tax-gatherers and others whom the lawyers and Pharisees thought were not worth talking to because they were so sinful. After telling the three stories Jesus said: 'There will be greater joy in heaven over one sinner who is sorry than over ninety-nine religious people who do not need to be sorry.'

Activities

Do the children know the meaning of 'sin' and 'sinner'? In groups, they could make lists of actions they think are sins. Which do they think is the worst sin? They could put their lists in order, beginning with the worst sin.

The children could make a collage of the angels in heaven, showing on one side their sadness at seeing people doing wrong, and on the other side their rejoicing over a sinner who repents. They could write about the sort of life 'sinners' had led, what they did and said to show their sorrow, and what they did to lead a better life.

Display

The chart displays the children's pictures of things they have lost and then found, and their writing about where they found them.

Resources

Bible (New Testament); works of art showing angels; blue, orange and yellow backing paper; white paper

There will be more Joy in Heaven over one sinner who repents...

Lost and found

Lost

Puma football. It has just signed a contract and you had better not let all of Currie in Lancs. (?)

Rolex watch (real, not fake)

Slipper. Lost on doorstep on Friday night. It had their name off when I fell. The wife beings on I wandered why my son was old.. Ella Owen, Lancs.

Barbie doll Angel Anne. Lost... on number 86 bus going to town and has blonde hair, blue eyes and is fair.

Dalmatian puppy, male (Ruff). Ruff is wearing a collar and a disc with his name, address and phone number.

Red Alfa Romeo, registration number ... Parked somewhere near Bootle station, but I can't remember where.

Reebok trainers, size 6. Left in Stanley Park on Sunday.

Sovereign ring Childwell area £10 reward.

Found

Fun fur Coat. Found in Calderstones Park on Saturday. Photograph in pocket. Label "St Michael" age 9-10.

Girl's hat and gloves, made of fake fur, black with wasps black and white. Found in Badgefield Town car park on Tuesday morning.

Phone handset found on hedge in Vauxfire Garden suburb Tuesday, Leece

Olympus Super zoom 70 af camera. Found outside Tesco Harlow on Monday. It has a film in it.

Two cats, one ginger, one striped, both male. The ginger one has a green ribbon. The striped one is black and grey, with a red ribbon, and a bell. They both have green eyes.

The lost son

There was once a man who had two sons; the younger was impatient to have his share of the family property. His father agreed to share his wealth between the two young men.

Before long the younger son had sold everything and was off to the big city to spend his money. It did not last long, especially when a famine struck the country. Soon he had no money left, not a penny, and so he had to find work. The only job he could find was looking after pigs; he was so hungry that he would have been glad to eat the pigs' food. Then he thought, "What am I doing here? I could be back in my father's house. I will go back and say I am sorry." The next day he set off for home.

His father saw him in the distance, and was overjoyed, and his heart went out to him, he ran to meet him, and flung his arms around his neck. ... is no longer fit to be called your son.

His father forgave him; he held a great feast to celebrate his homecoming. The elder brother was angry at all this fuss; he had always been a good son and nobody had celebrated that, but here was his no-good younger brother, home after spending all his money and everyone was ...

... His father said, " How could we help celebrating this happy day? You are always with me, and everything I have is yours. Your brother was dead and has come back to life, was lost and found."

Luke 15

Two cats, one ginger, one striped, both male. The ginger one has a green ribbon. The striped one is black and grey, with a red ribbon, and a bell. They both have green eyes.

# The Hindu scriptures

Background

The main Hindu scriptures are the *Vedas* (prayers and hymns); the *Brahmanas* (duties of Brahmins, or priests); the *Aranyakas* (religious teaching); and the *Upanishads* (Brahman and the soul). There are also stories: the *Mahabharata* and *Ramayana* (epic poems); the *Laws of Manu* (how to live); the *Puranas* (stories of the gods); and the *Vedanta Sutras* (philosophy). One story in the *Puranas* is about the god Krishna, whose birth is celebrated during the festival of Janmashtami.

Concepts

Sacred writings; symbols

Krishna being protected by a many-headed cobra

Story

A voice from the heavens spoke to Kansa, king of the Andhakaras: 'Your cousin Deviki's eighth child will kill you.' Deviki already had seven children. Her husband, Vasudeva, was from the Shoora family, who were enemies of the Andhakaras. Kansa was afraid, so he imprisoned Deviki and Vasudeva in his palace and had their seven children killed. Now it was near to the time when Deviki's eighth child would be born.

On the night the baby boy was born, people noticed the stars shining very brightly. Many thought it was a sign that something special had happened. Deviki knew that her baby, Krishna, had been born to fulfil a great destiny. 'How can we save him?' she wondered.

During the night a priest arrived at Deviki's cell with another baby. He said, 'Your friend Yashoda has sent her baby for you to keep in place of yours. Vasudeva, you must take Krishna to Yashoda's home.' Kansa heard about the birth of the baby and rushed to Deviki's cell. 'Where is Vasudeva?' he demanded, but Deviki would not speak.

Krishna grew up with Yashoda and her husband Nanda, who were cowherds. He spent his time with the milkmaids, making mischief and playing tricks on them. He was always forgiven because of his sweet nature, the beautiful music he played on his flute, and the heroic deeds he performed from an early age. Everyone knew he was special, a god.

Another voice spoke to Kansa, saying, 'He who will slay you is even now growing into manhood.' Kansa tricked Krishna into coming out of hiding. As Krishna travelled through the woods, he was attacked by demons sent by Kansa, but he overcame them all. Then Krishna fought a fierce battle with Kansa and won. Kansa lay dead, and Krishna had rid the world of evil. He later married Radha, one of the milkmaids.

Discussion

Talk about the characters in the story. The children could make lists of 'good' and 'evil' characters. How do they decide who is what?

Activities

The children could look at pictures of Krishna. What do they notice about him? His skin is very dark (sometimes shown as blue); he has a special mark on his forehead; he is often shown playing a flute; and a cow might be included in the picture. What shows that Krishna is special? Point out the halo around his head. The children could write a character study of Krishna, using reference books and pictures as sources.

Ask the children to find out about the tricks that Krishna played on the milkmaids. The children could retell and illustrate one of these.

Display

The children collaborated to make a poster-sized 'character study' of Krishna, which included a drawing based on illustrations in books. They also made 'book spines' on which they wrote the titles of the main Hindu scriptures, showing what each is about (see page 76).

Resources

Reference books about the Hindu scriptures; pictures and stories about the birth and childhood of Krishna; red and yellow backing paper

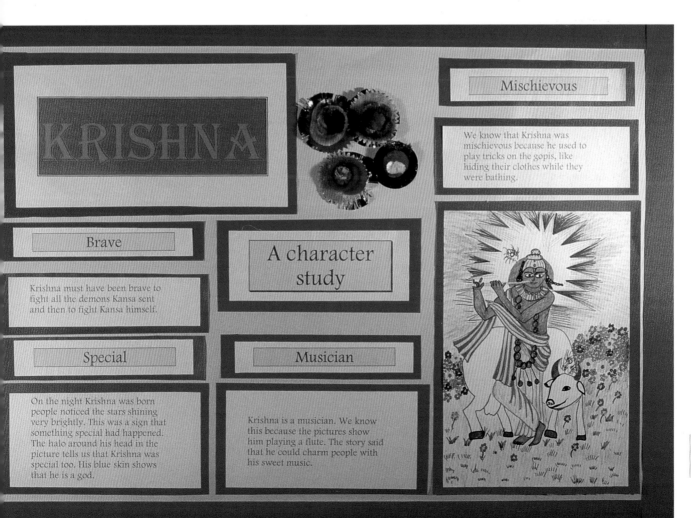

KRISHNA

A character study

Mischievous

We know that Krishna was mischievous because he used to play tricks on the gopis, like hiding their clothes while they were bathing.

Brave

Krishna must have been brave to fight all the demons Kansa sent and then to fight Kansa himself.

Special

On the night Krishna was born people noticed the stars shining very brightly. This was a sign that something special had happened. The halo around his head in the picture tells us that Krishna was special too. His blue skin shows that he is a god.

Musician

Krishna is a musician. We know this because the pictures show him playing a flute. The story said that he could charm people with his sweet music.

Joseph's dreams

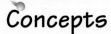

Concepts

Part of the Bible (the Old Testament) as Jewish as well as Christian scripture; signs and omens

Discussion

Ask the children if they would like to tell the class about dreams they have had. They could talk to a partner about other dreams. Can they think what has made them dream? The children might have dreamt about something they have done or are looking forward to, or something that has frightened them or is worrying them. Other dreams may seem to have no cause. The children might not have come across dreams with 'meanings'.

Story

Read a children's Bible version of the story of the two dreams that Joseph described to his brothers (Genesis 37: 5-11). What do the children think they mean?

Activities

The children could write descriptions of their dreams and illustrate them. Ask them to sort the dreams into different types, e.g. 'good times', 'bad times', 'things we look forward to', 'things that worry us'.

Read the story of the two dreams that were told to Joseph when he was imprisoned in a tower by the Pharaoh (Genesis 40).

Divide the children into two groups. Each group could read about one of the dreams that were told to Joseph in the tower. The children could write their own ideas about what the dream might have meant, before reading Joseph's explanation.

The children could research and write about Joseph's interpretation of Pharaoh's dreams (Genesis 41). They could then make 'lift-the-flap' books of the dreams that Joseph interpreted.

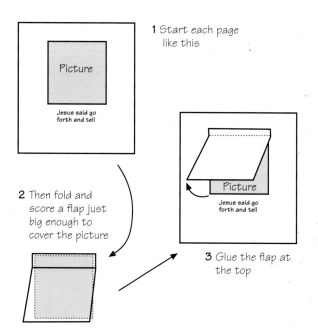

1 Start each page like this

2 Then fold and score a flap just big enough to cover the picture

3 Glue the flap at the top

Display

The background of bright blue and yellow represents the sky and sand of the countryside of the Bible lands. Joseph's coat is made from long strips of coloured paper and fabric, glued and stapled to a rough outline of a man. Some of the ends of the strips were left unfastened to allow movement. The letters of the heading were drawn with letter templates and then cut out. Joseph's dreams were copied on to 'speech bubbles' using brightly coloured felt-tipped pens.

Resources

Sky-blue and yellow backing paper; strips of brightly-coloured paper; white art paper; card; felt-tipped pens

Books for children

Folens Religious Education Pupil Books 1-4 (C Moorcroft, Folens 1995)
Junior Steps in RE Pupil Books Y3-Y6 (M & J Keene, Stanley Thornes 1997)
The Sleeping Beauty (Traditional, Ladybird 1993)
Badger's Parting Gifts (S Varley, Collins Picture Lions 1984)
Welcome to the Party (edited by S Roberts, BBC 1993)
A Child's Book of Prayer in Art (Sister Wendy Beckett, Dorling Kindersley)
Growing Up in Judaism (J Holm, Longman)
I am a Jew (C Lawton, Wayland)
World Religions: Hinduism (D Kadodwala, Wayland 1997)
World Religions: Judaism (A Wood, Wayland 1997)
World Religions: Islam (K Knight, Wayland 1997)
World Religions: Christianity (J Logan, Wayland 1997)
World Religions: Sikhism (K Kaur-Singh, Wayland 1997)
What Do We Know About Hinduism? (A Ganeri, Macdonald Young Books 1997)
What Do We Know About Judaism? (D Fine, Macdonald Young Books 1997)
My Buddhist Life (M St Pierre & M Casey, Wayland 1997)
My Christian Life (A Seaman, Wayland 1997)
My Hindu Life (D Kadodwala & S Chapi, Wayland 1997)
My Muslim Life (R El-droubie, Wayland 1997)
My Sikh Life (K Kaur-Singh, Wayland 1997)

Books for teachers

Folens Religious Education Teacher Books 1-4 (C Moorcroft, Folens 1995)
Stanley Thornes Infant RE (L Fidge & C Moorcroft, Stanley Thornes 1997)
Junior Steps in RE Teacher Books Y3-Y6 (M & J Keene, Stanley Thornes 1997)
Share Our World (J L Jackson, Stanley Thornes)
Red Letter Days (J L Jackson, Stanley Thornes)
Junior RE Handbook (R Jackson, Stanley Thornes)
A Gift to the Child (M Grimmitt, J Grove, J Hull & L Spencer, Simon & Schuster 1991)
Religious Education: Model Syllabuses - Questions and Teachings (SCAA 1994)
Religious Education: Model Syllabuses - Faith Communities' Working Group Reports (SCAA 1994)
Religious Education: Model Syllabuses - Glossary of Terms (SCAA 1994)
Folens Religious Education, Age 5-7 (P Emmett & S Hart 1993)
Teaching World Religions (C Erricker, Heinemann 1993)
How do I Teach RE? (G Read, J Rudge & R B Howarth, Stanley Thornes 1990)
The Effective Teaching of Religious Education (B Watson, Longman 1993)
The New English Bible (Oxford University Press 1970)
Priorities in Religious Education (B Watson, Falmer 1992)
Illuminated Manuscripts (D M Gill, Brockhampton Press 1996)
Festivals Together (S Fitzjohn, M Weston & J Large, Hawthorn Press 1993)
Ideas Bank: Islam (C Moorcroft, Folens 1995)
Ideas Bank: Hinduism (C Moorcroft, Folens 1995)
Ideas Bank: Festivals (E McCreery, L Prior and C Moorcroft, Folens 1995)
Ideas Bank: Judaism (L Prior, Folens 1995)
Ideas Bank: Christianity (E McCreery, Folens 1995)
Ideas Bank: Sikhism (L Prior, Folens 1995)
Photopack: Islam (D Rose, Folens 1995)
Examining Religions: Judaism (Ayre Forta, Heinemann 1993)
Getting Personal: Beginning Personal, Social and Health Education (C Moorcroft, Folens 1997)
The Alternative Service Book (HarperCollins Religious/ Cambridge University Press 1980)
Cruden's Concordance (Epworth Press 1948)
Good News Bible (Bible Society/HarperCollins 1994)

Suppliers of religious artefacts

TTS Religion in Evidence, Monk Road, Alfreton, Derbyshire, DE55 7RL
Articles of Faith, Bury Business Centre, Key Street, Bury, Lancs, BL9 6BU
Salvationist Publishing and Supplies Ltd, 117-121 Judd Street, King's Cross, London WC1H 9NN
'Little India', 91 The Broadway, Southall, Middlesex, UB1 1LN
Sikh Education Advisory Services, 9 Woodland Grove, Leeds, LS7 4HJ

Other suppliers

Wooden letter templates: John Lawrence Products, PO Box 77, Stowmarket, IP14 6SF

Useful organisations

The Shap Working Party, The National Society's RE Centre, 36 Causdon Street, London SW1P 4AU